Kaplan Publishing are constantly finding new ways to make a difference to your studies and our exciting online resources really do offer something different to students looking for exam success.

This book comes with free MyKaplan online resources so that you can study anytime, anywhere. **This free online resource is not sold separately and is included in the price of the book.**

Having purchased this book, you have access to the following online study materials:

CONTENT	AAT	
	Text	Kit
iPaper version of the book	✓	✓
Progress tests with instant answers	✓	
Mock assessments online	✓	✓
Material updates	✓	✓

How to access your online resources

Kaplan Financial students will already have a MyKaplan account and these extra resources will be available to you online. You do not need to register again, as this process was completed when you enrolled. If you are having problems accessing online materials, please ask your course administrator.

If you are already a registered MyKaplan user go to www.MyKaplan.co.uk and log in. Select the 'add a book' feature and enter the ISBN number of this book and the unique pass key at the bottom of this card. Then click 'finished' or 'add another book'. You may add as many books as you have purchased from this screen.

If you purchased through Kaplan Flexible Learning or via the Kaplan Publishing website you will automatically receive an e-mail invitation to MyKaplan. Please register your details using this email to gain access to your content. If you do not receive the e-mail or book content, please contact Kaplan Flexible Learning.

If you are a new user register at www.MyKaplan.co.uk and click on the link contained in the email we sent you to activate your account. Then select the 'add a book' feature, enter the ISBN number of this book and the unique pass key at the bottom of this card. Then click 'finished' or 'add another book'.

Your Code and Information

This code can only be used once for the registration of one book online. This registration and your online content will expire when the final sittings for the examinations covered by this book have taken place. Please allow one hour from the time you submit your book details for us to process your request.

D1422160

Please scratch the film to access your MyKaplan code.

Please be aware that this code is case-sensitive and you will need to include the dashes within the passcode, but not when entering the ISBN. For further technical support, please visit www.MyKaplan.co.uk

Professional Examinations

AQ2016

Using Accounting Software

EXAM KIT

This Exam Kit supports study for the following AAT qualifications:

AAT Foundation Certificate in Accounting – Level 2
AAT Foundation Diploma in Accounting and Business – Level 2
AAT Foundation Certificate in Bookkeeping – Level 2
AAT Level 2 Award in Accounting Skills to Run Your Business
AAT Foundation Certificate in Accounting at SCQF Level 5

KAPLAN

PUBLISHING

British Library Cataloguing-in-Publication Data

A catalogue record for this book is available from the British Library.

Published by:

Kaplan Publishing UK

Unit 2 The Business Centre

Molly Millar's Lane

Wokingham

Berkshire

RG41 2QZ

ISBN: 978-1-78415-588-9

© Kaplan Financial Limited, 2016

Printed and bound in Great Britain.

The text in this material and any others made available by any Kaplan Group company does not amount to advice on a particular matter and should not be taken as such. No reliance should be placed on the content as the basis for any investment or other decision or in connection with any advice given to third parties. Please consult your appropriate professional adviser as necessary. Kaplan Publishing Limited and all other Kaplan group companies expressly disclaim all liability to any person in respect of any losses or other claims, whether direct, indirect, incidental, consequential or otherwise arising in relation to the use of such materials.

CONTENTS

	Page
Index to practice questions	P.4
Exam technique	P.5
Paper specific information	P.6
Kaplan's recommended revision approach	P.7

Features in this exam kit

In addition to providing a wide ranging bank of real exam style questions, we have also included in this kit:

- Paper specific information and advice on exam technique.

- Our recommended approach to make your revision for this particular subject as effective as possible.

You will find a wealth of other resources to help you with your studies on MyKaplan and AAT websites:

www.mykaplan.co.uk

www.aat.org.uk/

Quality and accuracy are of the utmost importance to us so if you spot an error in any of our products, please send an email to mykaplanreporting@kaplan.com with full details, or follow the link to the feedback form in MyKaplan.

Our Quality Co-ordinator will work with our technical team to verify the error and take action to ensure it is corrected in future editions.

INDEX TO PRACTICE QUESTIONS

EXAM TECHNIQUE

- **Do not skip any of the material** in the syllabus.

- **Read each question** *very* carefully.

- **Double-check your answer** before committing yourself to it.

- Answer **every** question – if you do not know an answer to a multiple choice question or true/false question, you don't lose anything by guessing. Think carefully before you **guess**.

- If you are answering a multiple-choice question, **eliminate first those answers that you know are wrong**. Then choose the most appropriate answer from those that are left.

- **Don't panic** if you realise you've answered a question incorrectly. Getting one question wrong will not mean the difference between passing and failing

Computer-based exams – tips

- Do not attempt a CBA until you have **completed all study material** relating to it.

- On the AAT website there is a CBA demonstration. It is **ESSENTIAL** that you attempt this before your real CBA. You will become familiar with how to move around the CBA screens and the way that questions are formatted, increasing your confidence and speed in the actual exam.

- Be sure you understand how to use the **software** before you start the exam. If in doubt, ask the assessment centre staff to explain it to you.

- Questions are **displayed on the screen** and answers are entered using keyboard and mouse. At the end of the exam, you are given a certificate showing the result you have achieved.

- In addition to the traditional multiple-choice question type, CBAs will also contain **other types of questions**, such as number entry questions, drag and drop, true/false, pick lists or drop down menus or hybrids of these.

- In some CBAs you will have to type in complete computations or written answers.

- You need to be sure you **know how to answer questions** of this type before you sit the exam, through practice.

PAPER SPECIFIC INFORMATION

THE EXAM

FORMAT OF THE ASSESSMENT

The assessment will consist of one part and will cover the following areas:-

- **Enter accounting data at the beginning of an accounting period**

    Set up general ledger accounts, entering opening balances where appropriate.

    Set up customer accounts, entering opening balances where appropriate.

    Set up supplier accounts, entering opening balances where appropriate.

- **Record customer transactions**

    Process sales invoices and credit notes, accounting for VAT.

    Allocate monies received from customers in partial or full payment of invoices and balances.

- **Record supplier transactions**

    Process purchase invoices and credit notes, accounting for VAT.

    Allocate monies paid to suppliers in full or partial settlement of invoices and balances.

- **Record and reconcile bank and cash transactions**

    Process receipts and payments for non-credit transactions.

    Process recurring receipts and payments.

    Process petty cash receipts and payments, accounting for VAT.

    Perform a periodic bank reconciliation.

- **Be able to use journals for accounting transactions**

    Process journals for accounting transactions.

    Use journals to correct errors.

- **Produce reports**

    Produce routine reports for customers and suppliers.

    Produce routine reports from the general ledger.

Learners will be assessed by a computer based assessment, and will be required to demonstrate competence (70%).

Time allowed

2 hours

 Always keep your eye on the clock and make sure you attempt all questions!

KAPLAN'S RECOMMENDED REVISION APPROACH

QUESTION PRACTICE IS THE KEY TO SUCCESS

Success in professional examinations relies upon you acquiring a firm grasp of the required knowledge at the tuition phase. In order to be able to do the questions, knowledge is essential.

However, the difference between success and failure often hinges on your exam technique on the day and making the most of the revision phase of your studies.

The **Kaplan textbook** is the starting point, designed to provide the underpinning knowledge to tackle all questions. However, in the revision phase, poring over text books is not the answer.

The Kaplan workbook helps you consolidate your knowledge and understanding and is a useful tool to check whether you can remember key topic areas.

Kaplan pocket notes are designed to help you quickly revise a topic area, however you then need to practise questions. There is a need to progress to exam style questions as soon as possible, and to tie your exam technique and technical knowledge together.

The importance of question practice cannot be over-emphasised.

The recommended approach below is designed by expert tutors in the field, in conjunction with their knowledge of the examiner and the specimen assessment.

You need to practise as many questions as possible in the time you have left.

OUR AIM

Our aim is to get you to the stage where you can attempt exam questions confidently, to time, in a closed book environment, with no supplementary help (i.e. to simulate the real examination experience).

Practising your exam technique is also vitally important for you to assess your progress and identify areas of weakness that may need more attention in the final run up to the examination.

In order to achieve this we recognise that initially you may feel the need to practice some questions with open book help.

Good exam technique is vital.

THE KAPLAN CPAG REVISION PLAN

Stage 1: Assess areas of strengths and weaknesses

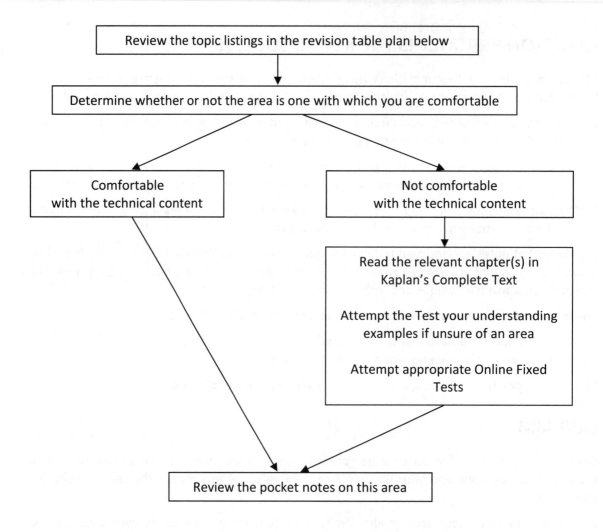

Stage 2: Practice questions

Follow the order of revision of topics as presented in this kit and attempt the questions in the order suggested.

Try to avoid referring to text books and notes and the model answer until you have completed your attempt.

Review your attempt with the model answer and assess how much of the answer you achieved.

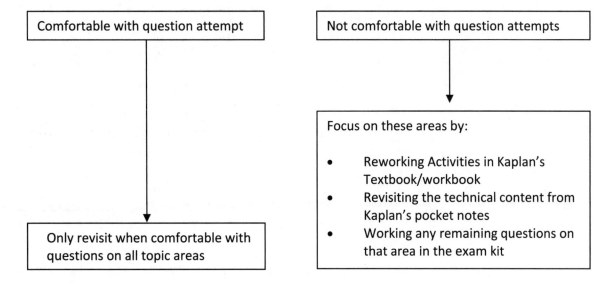

Stage 3: Final pre-exam revision

We recommend that you **attempt at least one two hour mock examination** containing a set of previously unseen exam standard questions.

Attempt the mock CBA online in timed, closed book conditions to simulate the real exam experience.

Section 1

PRACTICE QUESTIONS

PRACTICE PAPER 1

TOY SHOP

THE SITUATION

This assignment is based on an existing business, Toy Shop, a small manufacturer who has recently set up in business selling:

- Boxed Games
- Computer games
- Jigsaws

The owner of the business is James Free who operates as a sole trader.

At the start of the business James operated a manual bookkeeping system but has now decided that from 1st May 20XX the accounting system will become computerised.

You can assume that all documentation has been checked and authorised by James Free.

Some nominal ledger accounts have already been allocated suitable account codes. **You may need to amend or create other account codes.**

Set the company's Financial Year to start in May of the current year.

Their company details are:-

Toy Shop

64 Long Lane

Langhorne

North Yorkshire

YO21 3EJ

You are employed as an accounting technician.

The business is registered for VAT. The rate of VAT charged on all goods and services sold by Toy Shops is 20%.

TASK 1

Refer to the customer listing below and set up customer records to open Sales Ledger accounts for each customer.

Customer account code	Customer name, address and contact details	Customer account details
BB01	Busy Bee Toys 832 High Street Oxford OX2 3WG	Credit limit: £4000 Payment Terms: 30 days Opening Balance: £349.20 (relates to invoice 021 dated 12th Apr)
FF02	Forming Fun 21 Newton Quay Knott Mill Manchester M6 3RJ	Credit limit: £4000 Payment Terms: 30 days Opening Balance: £99.60 (relates to invoice 035 dated 8th Apr)
SM03	Space Models 13 Central Street Perth Scotland SC4 8RQ	Credit limit: £3000 Payment Terms: 30 days Opening Balance: £1195.20 (relates to invoice 093 dated 10th Apr)
TP04	Teddy T's Party 3 Paradise Street Wokingham WO4 6QP	Credit limit: £7000 Payment Terms: 30 days Opening Balance: £579.60 (relates to invoice 1003 dated 17th Apr)

TASK 2

Refer to the supplier listing below and set up supplier records to open Purchase Ledger accounts for each supplier.

Supplier account code	Supplier name, address and contact details	Supplier account details
PL01	Abacus C & C Unit 31 Kitts Industrial Estate St Helens Lancs	Credit limit: £5500 Payment Terms: 30 days Opening Balance: £369.60 (relates to invoice B/1874 dated 2nd Apr)
PL02	Compugames Ltd 6 Jury Road Dublin Eire	Credit limit: £4000 Payment Terms: 30 days Opening Balance: £511.20 (relates to invoice 1087 dated 11th Apr)
PL03	Space Models 13 Central Street Perth Scotland SC4 8RQ	Credit limit: £2000 Payment Terms: 30 days Opening Balance: £306 (relates to invoice F-0193 dated 18th Apr)
PL04	Toys Unlimited 95 Cuscaden Road Edinburgh Scotland	Credit limit: £2000 Payment Terms: 30 days Opening Balance: £970.80 (relates to invoice W/032 dated 18th Apr)

TASK 3.1

Refer to the list of General ledger balances below. Enter the opening balances onto the computerised accounting system, making sure you select the appropriate general ledger account codes.

List of general ledger balances as at the **1st May**

Account name	DR	CR
	£	£
Furniture and fixtures	5800.00	
Motor Vehicles	3000.00	
Bank	4225.00	
Petty Cash	300.00	
Sales Ledger Control Account *	2223.60	
Purchase Ledger Control Account *		2157.60
VAT on sales		543.00
VAT on purchases	109.00	
Capital		20000.00
Drawings	355.00	
Sales – Computer Games		6080.00
Sales – Jigsaws		700.00
Sales – Boxed Games		1967.00
Purchases – Computer Games	8000.00	
Purchases – Jigsaws	3200.00	
Purchases – Boxed Games	2465.00	
Office Stationery	53.00	
Electricity	167.00	
Rent and Rates	1550.00	
Note You do not need to enter these figures as you have already entered opening balances for customers and suppliers		

TASK 3.2

Transfer £500 from the bank current account to the bank deposit account. Enter this on the computerised accounting system using reference TRANS01 dated 1st May.

TASK 3.3

Print out the following reports and **identify and correct any errors**:

- Customer Address List
- Supplier Address List
- Trial Balance Report

TASK 4

Enter the following sales invoices and credit note onto the computerised accounting system.

	Toy Shops
	64 Long Lane
	Langhorne
	North Yorkshire
	YO21 3EJ
Telephone: 0121 765 3213	
Email: jp@toyshops.co.uk	
	Sales Invoice No 2021
	Date: 4th May 20XX

Busy Bee Toys	
832 High Street	
Oxford	
OX2 3WG	
Description	£
Computer Games	2585.00
VAT @ 20.00%	517.00
Total for payment	3102.00
	Terms 30 days

	Toy Shops
	64 Long Lane
	Langhorne
	North Yorkshire
	YO21 3EJ
Telephone: 0121 765 3213	
Email: jp@toyshops.co.uk	
	Sales Invoice No 2022
	Date: 4th May 20XX

Forming Fun	
21 Newton Quay	
Knott Mill	
Manchester	
M6 3RJ	
Description	£
Boxed Games	500.00
VAT @ 20.00%	100.00
Total for payment	600.00
	Terms 30 days

Toy Shops
64 Long Lane
Langhorne
North Yorkshire
YO21 3EJ

Telephone: 0121 765 3213
Email: jp@toyshops.co.uk

Sales Invoice No 2023

Date: 6th May 20XX

Teddy T's Party
3 Paradise Street
Wokingham
WO4 6QP

Description	£
Computer games	5000.00
VAT @ 20.00%	1000.00
Total for payment	6000.00

Terms 30 days

Toy Shops
64 Long Lane
Langhorne
North Yorkshire
YO21 3EJ

Telephone: 0121 765 3213
Email: jp@toyshops.co.uk

Credit Note No CN101

Date: 13th May 20XX

Teddy T's Party
3 Paradise Street
Wokingham
WO4 6QP

Description	£
Return faulty Computer games	320.00
VAT @ 20.00%	64.00
Total credit	384.00

TASK 5.1

Enter the following purchases invoices onto the computer system.

Date	A/C No.	Invoice Ref	Gross	Vat	Net	Computer games	Jigsaws	Boxed Games
3rd May	PL01	B/989	540.00	90.00	450.00	450.00		
5th May	PL02	145215	600.00	100.00	500.00			500.00
10th May	PL03	C-32632	1200.00	200.00	1000.00	1000.00		
10th May	PL04	12421	18.00	0.00	18.00		18.00	

TASK 5.2

Enter the following purchase credit note onto the computer system.

Date	Supplier	N/C	Credit Note Ref	Description	Details
15th May	Compugames	5000	11245	Computer Games	£88.00 Plus tax

TASK 6

The following remittance advices were received from customers. Enter the receipts onto the computerised accounting system.

Busy Bee Toys
Remittance Advice
To: Toy Shop Date: 17 May 20XX   A cheque for £349.20 (number 100322) is attached in payment of invoice no 021.

Forming Fun
Remittance Advice
To: Toy Shop Date: 17 May 20XX   A cheque for £99.60 (number 267543) is attached in payment of invoice 035.

Teddy T's Party	
BACS Remittance Advice	

To: Toy Shop

Date: 26 May 20XX

An amount of £195.60 has been paid directly into your bank account in payment of invoice 1003, including credit note CN101.

TASK 7

The following cheque payments were sent to suppliers; enter the payments on the accounts system. **Print off the relevant remittance advices**.

Date	Cheque No	Supplier	Amount	Details
22nd May	101333	Abacus C & C	369.60	Inv B/1874
22nd May	101334	Compugames	1005.60	Settle account in full.

TASK 8

Refer to the following cash sales and enter receipts into the computer. Use the bank current account for this transaction and enter 'cash sales' as the reference.

Date	Receipt Type	Gross	VAT	NET	Nominal code
13th May	Cash sale	1,200.00	200.00	1,000.00	4000
13th May	Cash sale	2,879.40	479.90	2,399.50	4001
20th May	Cash sale	995.00	0.00	995.00	4000

TASK 9

Enter the following petty cash payments onto the computerised accounting system.

Petty Cash Voucher			**Petty Cash Voucher**	
Date:	20.05.XX		**Date:**	21.05.XX
Voucher No:	012		**Voucher No:**	013
Details	£		**Details**	£
Subscriptions	32.00		Refreshments	10.40
(no Vat)			VAT	2.08
			Total	12.48
Authorised By;	*James Free*		**Authorised By;**	*James Free*
Receipt attached			Receipt attached	

TASK 10

Enter the following journal on the computerised accounting system.

Reference: JNL02			
Date	**Account Name & Code**	**Dr**	**Cr**
25th May	Drawings	2000.00	
	Bank		2000.00
Being the transfer of cash for James Free's personal use.			

TASK 11

Print out the following reports:

(a)   Trial Balance Report

(b)   Sales Day Book

(c)   Sales Returns Day Book

(d)   Purchase Day Book

(e)   Customer Activity Report

(f)   Supplier Activity Report

(g)   Aged Creditors Report

(h)   Aged Debtors Report

TASK 12

Refer to the following email below from James Free.

E-Mail
From: James Free **To:** Accounts Technician **Date:** 19th May 20XX **Subject:**
Hello A credit customer Forming Fun has moved premises. Their new address is as follows: 100 Aventi Way St Albans Hertfordshire AL2 4PM Please ensure that this is updated on the computerised accounts system. Thanks James

Create a screen shot of the customer's record with the new address and save it as a 'Word' document.

TASK 13

The sum of £502.00 has been incorrectly posted to the rent account instead of the electricity account in error. Process the following journal to correct this using reference JNL03. Use 31st May for the transaction.

Reference: JNL03			
Date	Account Name & Code	Dr	Cr
31st May	Electricity	502.00	
	Rent & Rates		502.00
Being the transfer of cash which was incorrectly posted to Rent instead of Electricity.			

TASK 14

The following cheque payments were sent to suppliers; enter the payments on the accounts system and **produce the relevant remittance advices**.

Date	Supplier	Cheque No	Details	Amount
28th May	Space Models	101335	Payment of opening balance	306.00
28th May	Toys Unlimited	101336	Part payment invoice W/032	450.00
28th May	Abacus C & C	BACS	Payment of invoice B/989	540.00

TASK 15

The following payments were received from customers; enter the receipts on the accounts system, dated 29 May 20XX.

Customer	Cheque No	Details	Amount (£)
Busy Bee	104662	Invoice 2021	3102.00
Forming Fun	828100	Part payment invoice 2022	400.00
Teddy T's Party	672522	Payment of invoice 2023	6000.00

TASK 16

On 14th May a member of staff buys Computer Games paying you £264.00 in Cash. This is inclusive of 20% VAT. Enter this in the bank current account and use reference CSH41 for this transaction.

TASK 17

On 19th May, you sold a 'Jigsaw' to a customer and they paid £45.00 (Zero rated VAT) debit card. Enter this in the bank current account and use reference 'Debit Card' for this transaction.

TASK 18

A cheque you received from Forming Fun for £99.60 (Cheque No 267543) has been returned by the bank marked 'Refer to Drawer – Insufficient Funds'. Process this returned cheque through the records, dated 17th May.

TASK 19

On the 5th May you are asked to set up a monthly recurring payment for a Direct Debit. It is to pay Insurance for £100.00 (Exempt VAT) for a period of 12 months commencing on 31st May. There is no VAT on this transaction. The Insurance is payable to Galloway Union. Provide evidence by taking a screen shot and saving it as a 'Word' document. Ensure you process this month's transaction.

TASK 20

You are asked to ensure that the petty cash account float is restored to a balance of £300.00 by bank transfer (dated 31st May). Enter this transaction onto the computerised system and use reference CSH25.

TASK 21

Toy Shop has been granted a bank loan for £10,000.00 and it has been received in to the bank current account on 31 May 20XX. Process the following journal to record this transaction (use ref JNL04).

Reference: JNL04			
Date	**Account Name & Code**	**Dr**	**Cr**
31st May	Bank Current Account	10000.00	
	Loan Account		10000.00
Being the proceeds received for a new loan.			

TASK 22

You are given the following bank statement and are asked to produce a bank reconciliation as at 31st May, processing any adjustments that may be necessary.

Friendly Bank plc

201 Main Road

Rochester

Kent

ME15 9JP

Toy Shops

64 Long Lane

Langthorne   31st May 20XX

North Yorkshire   Statement no: 0003

YO21 3EJ

Account number: 00678432

Statement of Account

Date: May 20XX	Details	Paid out £	Paid in £	Balance £
1 May	Opening balance			4225.00C
1 May	Transfer	500.00		3725.00C
13 May	Counter credit		1200.00	4925.00C
13 May	Counter credit		2879.40	7804.40C
14 May	Counter credit		264.00	8068.40C
17 May	Counter credit		349.20	8417.60C
17 May	Counter credit		99.60	8517.20C
19 May	Debit Card		45.00	8562.20C
20 May	Counter credit		995.00	9557.20C
22 May	Cheque 101333	369.60		9187.60C
23 May	Cheque 101334	1005.60		8182.00C
25 May	Counter debit Ref: JNL 02	2000.00		6182.00C
26 May	BACS: Teddy's T Party		195.60	6377.60C
28 May	Cheque 101336	450.00		5927.60C
29 May	Counter credit		3102.00	9029.60C
29 May	Counter credit		6000.00	15029.60C
29 May	Counter credit		400.00	15429.60C
30 May	BACS payment	540.00		14889.60C
31 May	Dishonoured cheque	99.60		14790.00C
31 May	Transfer	44.48		14745.52C
31 May	Direct Debit – Galloway Union	100.00		14645.52C
31 May	Bank charges	101.32		14544.20C
31 May	Loan		10000.00	24544.20C
	D = Debit C = Credit			

TASK 23

Print the following reports

(a)   Customer Activity (detailed) Report

(b)   Supplier Activity (detailed) Report

(c)   Period Trial Balance for the month of May

(d)   Audit Trail for May (detailed – transactions only including bank reconciled)

(e)   Aged Debtors (summary)

PRACTICE PAPER 2

CRAZY HAIR

THE SITUATION

This assignment is based on a new business, Crazy Hair, a small business recently set up to selling hair products.

The owner of the business is Nina Birk who operates as a sole trader.

At the start of the business Nina operated a manual bookkeeping system but has now decided that from 1st May 20XX the accounting system will become computerised.

You can assume that all documentation has been checked and authorised by Nina Birk.

Some nominal ledger accounts have already been allocated suitable account codes. **You may need to amend or create other account codes.**

Crazy Hair's financial year starts in May of the current year.

Their company details are:-
Crazy Hair
34 Clapham Road
Clapham
London
SE3 2HR

You are employed as an accounting technician.

The business is registered for VAT. The rate of VAT charged on all goods and services sold by Crazy Hair is 20%.

TASK 1

Refer to the customer listing below and set up customer records to open Sales Ledger accounts for each customer.

Customer account code	Customer name, address and contact details	Customer account details
104	Alfred Images Masuki Offices PO Box 5684 Birmingham B23 4RD	Credit limit: £8000 Payment Terms: 30 days Opening Balance: £1809.60 (relates to invoice 3352 dated 2nd April)
110	Figgaro Beta Studio 34 Knightsbridge Way Morden SE23 4KA	Credit limit: £6500 Payment Terms: 30 days Opening Balance: £3880.80 (relates to invoice 2856 dated 10th April)
118	Blades Alpha Studio 45 Key West London SE1 0JF	Credit limit: £6100 Payment Terms: 30 days Opening Balance: £2144.40 (relates to invoice 3345 dated 18th April)
122	Hair Studio Framlington Court Lee London SE4 7YH	Credit limit: £5000 Payment Terms: 30 days Opening Balance: £681.60 (relates to invoice 3098 dated 12th April)
138	Ribbons & Curls PO Box 1120 Canning Town London TN2 2EB	Credit limit: £5000 Payment Terms: 30 days Opening Balance: £391.20 (relates to invoice 3123 dated 12th April)

TASK 2

Refer to the supplier listing below and set up supplier records to open Purchase Ledger accounts for each supplier.

Supplier account code	Supplier name, address and contact details	Supplier account details
1134	Avada Cash & Carry 32 Surrey Quay Isle of Dogs E12 3NW	Credit limit: £5500 Payment Terms: 30 days Opening Balance: £4454.40 (relates to invoice C/251 dated 22nd April)
1138	Straightside Supplies Havering Place Holborn London WC1 2PP	Credit limit: £12000 Payment Terms: 30 days Opening Balance: £1839.60 (relates to invoice 9140 dated 11th April)
1165	Hair Supplies 43 St Helens Way London SE7 3RF	Credit limit: £4000 Payment Terms: 30 days Opening Balance: £818.40 (relates to invoice 0028 dated 11th April)
1185	Wig Specialists Retro Square 32 Wigmore Road London EC1V 3SG	Credit limit: £5000 Payment Terms: 30 days Opening Balance: £102.00 (relates to invoice S653 dated 18th April)

TASK 3.1

Refer to the list of General ledger balances below. Enter the opening balances into the computer, making sure you select the appropriate general ledger account codes.

List of general ledger balances as at the **1st May**

Account name	£	£
Motor Vehicle	24000.00	
Furniture and Fixtures	31000.00	
Bank	54210.81	
Petty Cash	200.00	
Sales Ledger Control Account *	8907.60	
Purchase Ledger Control Account*		7214.40
VAT on Sales		5550.00
VAT on Purchases	1507.94	
Capital		165000.00
Drawings	5000.00	
Sales – Brushes		345.00
Sales – Combs		187.00
Sales – Colours		3801.45
Sales – Hairdryers		758.00
Sales – Wigs		5600.00
Cash Sales		617.50
Purchases – Brushes	873.00	
Purchases – Combs	50.00	
Purchases – Colour	4200.00	
Purchases – Hairdryers	6310.00	
Purchases – Wigs	52814.00	
*Note You do not need to enter these figures as you have already entered opening balances for customers and suppliers.		

TASK 3.2

Print out the following reports and **identify and correct any errors**:

(a)   Customer Address List

(b)   Supplier Address List

(c)   Trial Balance

TASK 4

Enter the following sales invoices onto the computer.

Crazy Hair
34 Clapham Road
Clapham
London
SE3 2HR

Account No: 138
Invoice No: 3353

Date: 12 May 20XX

Ribbons & Curls
PO Box 1120
Canning Town
London
TN2 2EB

Quantity	Description	Unit Price	Net Cost	Tax	Gross	Nominal code
10	Colours	14.10	141.00	28.20	169.20	4002

Terms 30 days

Crazy Hair
34 Clapham Road
Clapham
London
SE3 2HR

Account No: 104
Invoice No: 3354

Date: 12 May 20XX

Alfred Images
Masuki Offices
PO Box 5684
Birmingham
B23 4RD

Quantity	Description	Unit Price	Net Cost	Tax	Gross	Nominal code
50	Brushes	11.62	581.00	116.20	697.20	4000

Terms 30 days

Crazy Hair
34 Clapham Road
Clapham
London
SE3 2HR

Account No: 110
Invoice No: 3355

Date: 13th May 20XX

Figgaro
Beta Studio
34 Knightsbridge Way
Morden
SE23 4KA

Quantity	Description	Unit Price	Net Cost	Tax	Gross	Nominal code
12	Hairdryers	55.00	660.00	132.00	792.00	4003

Terms 30 days

Crazy Hair
34 Clapham Road
Clapham
London
SE3 2HR

Account No: 118
Invoice No: 3356

Date: 15th May 20XX

Blades
Alpha Studio
45 Key West
London
SE1 0JF

Quantity	Description	Unit Price	Net Cost	Tax	Gross	Nominal code
8	Wigs	210.72	1685.76	337.15	2022.91	4004
3	Hairdryers	67.80	203.40	40.68	244.08	4003

Terms 30 days

Crazy Hair
34 Clapham Road
Clapham
London
SE3 2HR

Account No: 122
Invoice No: 3357

Date: 18 May 20XX

Hair Studio
Framlington Court
Lee
London
SE4 7YH

Quantity	Description	Unit Price	Net Cost	Tax	Gross	Nominal code
12	Brushes	26.40	316.80	63.36	380.16	4000
4	Wigs	220.48	881.92	176.38	1058.30	4004
16	Colours	14.40	230.40	46.08	276.48	4002

Terms 30 days

TASK 5

On 25th May you send a credit note (CN23) to Alfred Images (Account No 104) for brushes.

The total is £67.20 which includes tax.

TASK 6

Enter the purchases invoices into the computer.

Date	A/C No.	Invoice Ref	Description	Nominal Code	Net	Vat	Gross
11 May	1138	3362	Brushes	5000	191.60	38.32	229.92
11 May	1134	C/910	Colours	5002	954.00	190.80	1144.80
13 May	1165	0814	Hairdryers	5003	178.56	0.00	178.56
14 May	1185	S1198	Wigs	5004	3393.60	678.72	4072.32

TASK 7

Enter the following purchase credit note onto the computer system.

Date	A/C No	Supplier	N/C	Credit Note Ref	Amount
18 May	1185	Wigs Specialist	5004	C3223	123.24 Including Vat

TASK 8

The following payments were received from customers; enter the receipts on the accounts system.

Date	Receipt type	Customer	Amount	Details
20 May	Cheque No: 183001	Alfred Images	1809.60	Payment for invoice 3352
21 May	Cheque No: 654255	Blades	2144.40	Payment for invoice 3345
21 May	BACS	Figgaro	3880.80	Payment for invoice 2856
21 May	Cheque No: 452221	Hair Studio	681.60	Payment for invoice 3098

TASK 9

The following cheque payments were sent to suppliers; enter the payments on the accounts system dated 31st May and **produce the relevant remittance advices**.

Supplier	Cheque No:	Amount	Details
Wigs Specialist	163455	£102.00	Payment for invoice S653
Avada Cash & Carry	163456	£4454.40	Payment for invoice C/251
Hair Supplies	163457	£818.40	Payment for invoice 0028

TASK 10

Enter the following petty cash payments into the computer:

Date	Ref	Nominal Code	Net	VAT	Gross
19 May	CSH 86	7400	33.60	6.72	40.32
20 May	CSH 87	7500	4.51	0.00	4.51

TASK 11

On the 20th May, a member of staff purchases a 'Brush' from you and pays Crazy Hair a total of £21.00 in cash. This is inclusive of VAT of £3.50. Enter this in the bank current account and use reference 1001 for this transaction.

TASK 12

Print out the following reports:

(a)   Trial Balance Report

(b)   Sales Day Book

(c)   Sales Returns Day Book

(d)   Purchase Day Book

(e)   Customer Activity Report

(f)   Supplier Activity Report

(g)   Aged Creditors Report (summary)

(h)   Aged Debtors Report (summary)

TASK 13

Enter the following journal

<table>
<tr><td colspan="4" align="center">Ref : JH12</td></tr>
<tr><td>Date</td><td>Account Name & Code</td><td>Dr</td><td>Cr</td></tr>
<tr><td>24 May</td><td>Drawings</td><td>440.00</td><td></td></tr>
<tr><td></td><td>Bank</td><td></td><td>440.00</td></tr>
<tr><td colspan="4">Being the transfer of cash for personal use.</td></tr>
</table>

TASK 14

(a)   Refer to the following email below from Frances Williams

<table>
<tr><td align="center">**E-Mail**</td></tr>
<tr><td>From: Frances Williams
Date: 19th May 20XX
Subject: Customer change of address</td></tr>
<tr><td>Hello

A credit customer Ribbons and Curls has moved premises. New address as follows:
122 Devonshire Road
Cranbrook
London
SE1 2AB
Please ensure that this is updated on the computerised accounts system.

Thanks
Frances</td></tr>
</table>

(b)   **Create a screen shot** of the customer's record showing the change of address and save it as a 'Word' document. Use a suitable file name to save the document.

TASK 15

A cheque you received from Hair Studio for £681.60 (Cheque No 452221) has been returned by the bank marked 'Refer to Drawer – Insufficient Funds'. Process this returned cheque through the records, dated 21st May.

TASK 16

On 31st May you transfer £30.52 from the Bank account to the petty cash account. Use reference TRF01.

TASK 17

You are given the following bank statement and are asked to produce a bank reconciliation at 31st May, processing any adjustments that may be necessary. Ensure that the direct debit for Coopers Union is coded to Premises Insurance costs. There is no VAT applicable on both direct debits.

Nice Bank plc
201 Main Road
Rochester
Kent
ME15 9JP

Crazy Hair
34 Clapham Road
London
SE3 2HR

31st May 20XX
Statement no: 0012

Account number: 32543211

Statement of Account

Date: May 20XX	Details	Paid out £	Paid in £	Balance £
01 May	Opening balance			54210.81C
14 May	Counter credit		1809.60	56020.41C
20 May	Counter credit		2144.40	58164.81C
20 May	BACS		3880.80	62045.61C
20 May	Counter credit		681.60	62727.21C
20 May	Counter credit		21.00	62748.21C
24 May	Dishonoured cheque	681.60		62066.61C
24 May	Counter Debit	440.00		61626.61C
24 May	Direct Debit – Coopers Union	168.00		61458.61C
24 May	Counter Debit	30.52		61428.09C
31 May	Direct Debit – Electricity	66.94		61361.15C
31 May	Bank Charges	27.11		61334.04C
	D = Debit C = Credit			

TASK 18

Print the following reports

(a)   Customer Address List

(b)   Customer Activity

(c)   Supplier Activity

(d)   Trial Balance for the month of May (include opening balances)

(e)   Audit Trail for May only (summary)

(f)   Aged Creditors (summary)

(g)   Aged Debtors (summary)

(h)   Nominal Ledger Activity Report for the following accounts

     1.1.1.   Bank Current Account

     1.1.2.   Petty Cash Account

PRACTICE PAPER 3

SHOES 4U

THE SITUATION

This assignment is based on an existing organisation, Shoes 4U, a small business selling ladies and men's shoes.

The owner of the business is Dennis Cope who operates as a sole trader.

At the start of the business Dennis operated a manual bookkeeping system but has now decided that from 1st June 20XX the accounting system will become computerised.

You can assume that all documentation has been checked by Dennis Cope.

Some nominal ledger accounts have already been allocated suitable account codes. **You may need to amend or create other account codes.**

Shoes 4U's financial year starts in June of the current year.

Their company details are:-

Shoes 4U

85 Barrington Close

Carlisle

Cumbria

C41 3ED

You are employed as an accounting technician.

The business is registered for VAT. The rate of VAT charged on all goods and services sold by Shoes 4U is 20%.

TASK 1

Refer to the customer listing below and set up customer records to open Sales Ledger accounts for each customer.

Customer account code	Customer name, address and contact details	Customer account details
SL186	Beckers Gate Ltd Butchergate Carlisle Cumbria C41 1SG	Credit limit: £5000 Payment Terms: 30 days Opening Balance: £4811.88 (relates to invoice 1613 dated 22nd May)
SL213	Eaton Bowls Club Seaton Street St Neots Cambs PE19 8EF	Credit limit: £3000 Payment Terms: 30 days Opening Balance: £961.98 (relates to invoice 1582 dated 10th May)
SL302	Jones Footwear Scotby Village Carlisle Cumbria C44 8BP	Credit limit: £6000 Payment Terms: 30 days Opening Balance: £3828.75 (relates to invoice 1596 dated 28th May)
SL307	Dickens Ladies Footwear 17 Royal Square Bleachfield North Yorkshire YO87 9AD	Credit limit: £11000 Payment Terms: 30 days Opening Balance: £783.66 (relates to invoice 1601 dated 21st May)

TASK 2

Refer to the supplier listing below and set up supplier records to open Purchase Ledger accounts for each supplier.

Supplier account code	Supplier name, address and contact details	Supplier account details
PL112	Bootsy & Smudge Ltd Factory Road Stilton Cambs PE7 3RP	Credit limit: £4000 Payment Terms: 30 days Opening Balance: £2881.26 (relates to invoice B/468 dated 22nd May)
PL168	Briggsthorpe Boots Long Buckby Wharf Long Buckby Northampton NN4 9UW	Credit limit: £50000 Payment Terms: 30 days Opening Balance: £43200.00 (relates to invoice 0001087 dated 18th May)
PL172	Gallows Fashion 18 The Crescent Pickford Cambs PE7 8QV	Credit limit: £2000 Payment Terms: 30 days Opening Balance: £400.00 (relates to invoice G-01239 dated 16th May)
PL173	Dickens Ladies Footwear 17 Royal Square Bleachfield North Yorkshire YO87 9AD	Credit limit: £2000 Payment Terms: 30 days Opening Balance: £567.00 (relates to invoice 06345 dated 16th May)

TASK 3.1

Refer to the list of General ledger balances below. Enter the opening balances into the computer, making sure you select the appropriate general ledger account codes.

List of general ledger balances as at the 1st June

Account name	£	£
Freehold Property	72000.00	
Motor Vehicles	7500.00	
Furniture and Fixtures	9000.00	
Bank	19363.00	
Petty Cash	200.00	
Sales Ledger Control *	10386.27	
Purchase Ledger Control *		47048.26
VAT on Sales		3402.35
VAT on Purchases	1130.00	
Capital		30000.00
Drawings	600.00	
Sales – Men's Footwear		79320.00
Sales – Ladies Footwear		43210.00
Cash Sales		6798.00
Purchases – Men's Footwear	55432.00	
Purchases – Ladies Footwear	23410.00	
Advertising	7231.00	
Telephone	866.00	
Rent	1263.00	
Electricity	567.34	
Office Stationery	830.00	
Note You do not need to enter these figures as you have already entered opening balances for customers and suppliers		

TASK 3.2

Transfer £5000 from the bank current account to the bank deposit account, dated 1st June. Use TRF01 as the reference.

TASK 3.3

Print out the following reports and identify and correct any errors:

(a)   Customer Address list

(b)   Supplier Address List

(c)   Period Trial Balance Report

TASK 4

Enter the following sales invoices and credit notes on to the computer.

Shoes 4u
85 Barrington Close
Carlisle
Cumbria
C41 3ED

Sales Invoice No: 1622
Date: 4th June 20XX

Becker Gate Ltd
Butchergate
Carlisle
Cumbria
C41 1SG

Description	£
Men's Footwear	450.00
VAT @ 20.00%	90.00
Total for payment	540.00

Terms 30 days

Shoes 4u
85 Barrington Close
Carlisle
Cumbria
C41 3ED

Sales Invoice No: 1623
Date: 6th June 20XX

Eaton Bowls Club
Seaton Street
St Neots
Cambs
PE19 8EF

Description	£
Men's Footwear	1385.00
VAT @ 20.00%	277.00
Total for payment	1662.00

Terms 30 days

Shoes 4u
85 Barrington Close
Carlisle
Cumbria
C41 3ED

Sales Invoice No: 1624
Date: 14th June 20XX

Dickens Ladies Footwear
17 Royal Square
Bleachfield
North Yorkshire
YO87 9AD

Description	£
Men's Footwear	450.00
Ladies Footwear	1850.00
VAT @ 20.00%	460.00
Total for payment	2760.00

Terms 30 days

Shoes 4u
85 Barrington Close
Carlisle
Cumbria
C41 3ED

Sales Invoice No: 1625
Date: 17th June 20XX

Jones Footwear
Scotby Village
Carlisle
Cumbria
C44 8BP

Description	£
Ladies Footwear	1175.75
VAT @ 20.00%	235.15
Total for payment	1410.90

Terms 30 days

Shoes 4u
85 Barrington Close
Carlisle
Cumbria
C41 3ED

Credit Note No: CR10
Date: 8th June 20XX

Dickens Ladies Footwear

17 Royal Square

Bleachfield

North Yorkshire

YO87 9AD

Description	£
Returned Ladies Footwear – Damage in transit	235.00
VAT @ 20.00%	47.00
Total for payment	282.00

Terms 30 days

TASK 5

Enter supplier invoices into the computer.

Date	Description	N/C	Invoice Ref	Net	Vat	Gross
2 June	Bootsy & Smudge Ltd	5001	B/752	300.00	60.00	360.00
10 June	Briggsthorpe Boots	5000	12350	2500.00	500.00	3000.00
12 June	Gallows Fashion	5000	G-2285	2500.00	500.00	3000.00
13 June	Bootsy & Smudge Ltd	5001	B/753	200.00	40.00	240.00

TASK 6

The following payments were received from customers; enter the receipts on the accounts system.

Date	A/c No	Customer	Cheque No	Details	Amount £
11 June	SL186	Beckers Gate Ltd	199846	Payment for invoice 1613	4811.88
14 June	SL213	Eaton Bowls Club	107654	Payment for invoice 1582	961.98
14 June	SL302	Jones Footwear	244536	Payment for invoice 1596	3828.75

TASK 7

The following cheque payments were sent to suppliers; enter the payments on the accounts system and **raise the relevant remittance advices**.

Date	A/c No	Supplier	Cheque No	Details	Amount £
18 June	PL172	Gallows Fashion	109887	Payment for invoice G-01239	400.00
18 June	PL168	Briggsthorpe Boots	109888	Part Payment for invoice 0001087	23300.00

TASK 8.1

The following items were paid by cash

Petty Cash Voucher		
Date:		05.06.XX
Voucher No:		010
Details		£
Refreshments *(no Vat)*		9.90
Authorised By;		*Dennis Cope*
Receipt attached		

Petty Cash Voucher		
Date:		10.06.XX
Voucher No:		011
Details		£
Office stationery		11.25
VAT		2.25
Total		13.50
Authorised By;		*Dennis Cope*
Receipt attached		

TASK 8.2

Reimburse the petty cash tin with £23.40 which has been withdrawn from the bank. Use 10th June 20XX and reference TRF02 for this transaction.

TASK 9

On the 23rd June, a member of staff purchases 'Mens Footwear' from you and pays you a total of £77.59 in cash. This is inclusive of VAT. Enter this in to the bank current account and use reference F027 for the transaction.

TASK 10

Print out the following reports:

(1)   Trial Balance Report

(2)   Sales Day Book

(3)   Customer Activity Report

(4)   Supplier Activity Report

(5)   Aged Creditors Report (detailed)

(6)   Aged Debtors Report (detailed)

(7)   Nominal Ledger Activity Report for the following accounts

      (a)   Bank Current Account

      (b)   Petty Cash Account

TASK 11.1

Refer to the following standing order schedule:

- Set up a recurring entry as shown in the standing order schedule below.
- **Print a screen shot** of the screen setting up the recurring entry.
- Process the first payment.

Details	Amount	Frequency of payment	Total number of payments	Payment start date 20XX	Payment finish date 20XX
Electricity (ECBE Ltd)	£193.00 No Vat	Quarterly	4	25th June 20XX	25th March 20XX

TASK 11.2

Refer to the following BACS receipt schedule:

- Set up a recurring entry as shown in the schedule below.
- **Print a screen shot** of the screen setting up the recurring entry.
- Process the first receipt.

Details	Amount	Frequency of receipt	Total number of receipts	Start date 20XX	Finish date 20XX
Rent	£1500 (no VAT)	Quarterly	4	30th June 20XX	30th March 20XX

TASK 12

Enter the following journal.

JOURNAL No: 209			
Date	Account Name & Code	Dr	Cr
25th June	Drawings	3200.00	
	Bank		3200.00
Being the transfer of cash for personal use.			

TASK 13

On 22nd June you sold Ladies Footwear to a customer and they paid £54.00 debit card inclusive of tax £9.00. Use reference DC03.

TASK 14

A cheque you received from Eaton Bowls Club for £961.98 (Cheque no: 107654) has been returned by the bank marked 'Refer to Drawer – Insufficient Funds'. Process this returned cheque through the records, dated 14th June.

TASK 15

Refer to the following email below from Dennis Cope.

E-Mail
From: Dennis Cope
To: Accounts Technician
Date: 30th June 20XX
Subject: Customer write off
Hello In view of Eaton Bowls Club and cheque that was returned by their bankers, I have decided that we should write off the **balance of their account** at 30th June 20XX. Please ensure that this is done. Thanks Dennis Cope

TASK 16

You are given the following bank statement and are asked to produce a bank reconciliation at 30th June 20XX, processing any adjustments that may be necessary. The BACS receipt on the 25th June relates to Rent Received.

Friendly Bank plc

201 Lake Rise
Whitewater
Cumbria
C21 9JF

STATEMENT : ACCOUNT No 22567767

Shoes 4U	30th June 20XX
85 Barrington Close	Statement 0011
Carlisle	
Cumbria	
C41 3ED	

Date June 20XX	Detail	Paid out £	Paid in £	Balance
1st June	Opening Balance			19363.00C
1st June	Transfer	5000.00		14363.00C
14th June	Counter debit	23.40		14339.60C
14th June	Cheque receipt		4811.88	19151.48C
14th June	Cheque receipt		961.98	20113.46C
16th June	Dishonoured Cheque	961.98		19151.48C
18th June	Cheque 109888	23300.00		4148.52D
21st June	Debit Card transaction		54.00	4094.52D
22nd June	DD – ECBE Ltd	193.00		4287.52D
23rd June	Counter credit		77.59	4209.93D
25th June	Counter Debit	3200.00		7409.93D
25th June	Bank Charges	50.00		7459.93D
30th June	Counter Credit		3828.75	3631.18D
30th June	BACS receipt		1500.00	2131.18D

C = Credit	D = Debit	DD – Direct Debit

TASK 17

Print the following reports:

(1)   Trial Balance for the month of June (Inc. opening balances)

(2)   Detailed Audit Trail (including bank reconciled items)

(3)   Nominal Ledger Activity Report for the following accounts:

   (a)   Trade Creditors

   (b)   Sales – Ladies Footwear

(4)   Aged Debtors Analysis (detailed)

PRACTICE PAPER 4

SPORTS GEAR

THE SITUATION

This assignment is based on an existing business, **Sports Gear**, who has recently set up in business selling sports equipment.

The owner of the business is Nina Birk who operates as a sole trader.

At the start of the business Nina operated a manual bookkeeping system but has now decided that from 1st July 20XX the accounting system will become computerised.

You can assume that all documentation has been checked and authorised by Nina Birk.

Some nominal ledger accounts have already been allocated suitable account codes. **You may need to amend or create other account codes.**

Sport Gear's Financial Year starts in July.

Their company details are:-

Sports Gear

34 Hockey Avenue

Tennison

London

EC1V 1NY

You are employed as an accounting technician.

The business is registered for VAT. The rate of VAT charged on all goods and services sold by Sports Gear is 20%.

TASK 1

Refer to the customer listing below and set up customer records to open Sales Ledger accounts for each customer.

Customer account code	Customer name, address and contact details	Customer account details
SL01	J Hollingham 56 Glencoe Avenue Gants Hill Ilford Essex IG1 6FR	Credit limit: £5000 Payment Terms: 30 days Opening Balance: £3462.12 (relates to invoice 1001 dated 12th June 20XX)
SL02	Paul McCallum 34 St Albans Road Seven Kings Essex IG7 8DS	Credit limit: £9500 Payment Terms: 30 days Opening Balance: £514.68 (relates to invoice 0087 dated 10th June 20XX)
SL03	Kerry Jenkins 34 Gloucester Road Gillingham Kent ME14 3TL	Credit limit: £8000 Payment Terms: 30 days Opening Balance: £758.34 (relates to invoice 0093 dated 8th June 20XX)
SL04	Harry Bucket 54 Dale Road Harrogate North Yorks Y02 3HN	Credit limit: £12000 Payment Terms: 30 days Opening Balance: £2767.34 (relates to invoice 1003 dated 12th June 20XX)
SL05	Evelyn Rose 98 Crabtree Drive Bromley Kent DA3 6AY	Credit limit: £7000 Payment Terms: 30 days Opening Balance: £942.98 (relates to invoice 1004 dated 12th June 20XX)

TASK 2

Refer to the supplier listing below and set up supplier records to open Purchase Ledger account for each supplier.

Supplier account code	Supplier name, address and contact details	Supplier account details
PL01	Radcliff and Sons Orient House Lower Clapham London E1 2RH	Credit limit: £15500 Payment Terms: 30 days Opening Balance: £5362.14 (relates to invoice 1874 dated 22nd June 20XX)
PL02	Tennison Bros White Cottage London WC1 6YD	Credit limit: £11000 Payment Terms: 30 days Opening Balance: £2801.00 (relates to invoice B-321 dated 11th June 20XX)
PL03	Skipton & Co 22 Chatsworth Lane Water Square London EC1V 6NJ	Credit limit: £9000 Payment Terms: 30 days Opening Balance: £501.00 (relates to invoice 1087 dated 11th June 20XX)
PL04	Evelyn Rose 98 Crabtree Drive Bromley Kent DA3 6AY	Credit limit: £3000 Payment Terms: 30 days Opening Balance: £250.00 (relates to invoice A193 dated 18th June 20XX)

TASK 3.1

Refer to the list of General ledger balances below. Enter the opening balances into the computer, making sure you select the appropriate general ledger account codes.

List of general ledger balances as at 01.07.20XX

Account name	£	£
Motor Vehicle	15500.00	
Furniture and Fixtures	18000.00	
Office Equipment	8430.00	
Bank	3325.40	
Petty Cash	300.00	
Sales Ledger Control Account*	8445.46	
Purchase Ledger Control Account*		8914.14
VAT on Sales		3458.00
VAT on Purchases	1120.00	
Capital		52000.00
Drawings	1294.00	
Sales – Tennis Racquets		13266.78
Sales – Exercise Bikes		22310.00
Sales – Golf Clubs		9543.00
Sales – Fishing Rods		5644.00
Purchases – Tennis Racquets	21354.00	
Purchases – Exercise Bikes	25610.00	
Purchases – Golf Clubs	5475.00	
Purchases – Fishing Rods	4796.00	
Office Stationery	430.00	
Postage	560.00	
Electricity	496.06	
Note You do not need to enter these figures as you have already entered opening balances for customers and suppliers		

TASK 3.2

Print out the following reports and **identify and correct any errors:**

> Customer Address list
>
> Supplier Address List
>
> Period Trial Balance Report

TASK 4

Enter the following sales invoices and credit notes onto the computer.

INVOICE
Sports Gear
34 Hockey Avenue
Tennison
London
EC1V 1NY

Account No: SL01   Date: 4 July 20XX
Invoice No: 1052

J Hollingham
56 Glencoe Avenue
Gants Hill
Ilford
Essex
IG1 6FR

Quantity	Description	Unit Price	Net £	Tax £	Gross £	Nominal code
20	Tennis Racquets	44.10	882.00	176.40	1058.40	4000
10	Exercise Bikes	102.36	1023.60	204.72	1228.32	4001
6	Fishing Rods	54.00	324.00	64.80	388.80	4003

Terms 30 days

INVOICE
Sports Gear
34 Hockey Avenue
Tennison
London
EC1V 1NY

Account No: SL03   Date: 6 July 20XX
Invoice No: 1053

Kerry Jenkins
Gloucester Road
Gillingham
Kent
ME14 3TL

Quantity	Description	Unit Price	Net £	Tax £	Gross £	Nominal code
3	Tennis Racquets	44.10	132.30	26.46	158.76	4000

Terms 30 days

INVOICE

Sports Gear
34 Hockey Avenue
Tennison
London
EC1V 1NY

Account No: SL04   Date: 8 July 20XX
Invoice No: 1054

Harry Bucket
54 Dale Road
Yorkshire
Y02 3HN

Quantity	Description	Unit Price	Net £	Tax £	Gross £	Nominal code
18	Golf Clubs	84.10	1513.80	302.76	1816.56	4002

Terms 30 days

CREDIT NOTE

Sports Gear
34 Hockey Avenue
Tennison
London
EC1V 1NY

Account No: SL01   Date: 17 July 20XX
Invoice No: CR34

J Hollingham
56 Glencoe Avenue
Gants Hill
Ilford
Essex
IG1 6FR

Description	£
Return faulty Exercise Bike	510.63
VAT @ 20.0%	102.12
Total credit	612.75

TASK 5

Enter the purchases invoices into the computer.

Date	A/C No.	Invoice Ref	Description	Net	Vat	Gross	Nominal code
3 July	PL01	1099	Tennis Racquets	550.00	110.00	660.00	5000
5 July	PL02	B – 1147	Exercise Bikes	320.00	64.00	384.00	5001
5 July	PL02	B – 1147	Postage	35.00	0.00	35.00	7803
10 July	PL03	2785	Golf Clubs	938.00	187.60	1125.60	5002
10 July	PL04	A/5698	Fishing Rods	671.00	134.20	805.20	5003

TASK 6

On 19th July, you receive a credit note (CX432) from Skipton & Co (Account No PL03) for two Golf Clubs that had been returned to them. The total credit note is for 109.45 plus sales tax of 20%.

TASK 7

The following payments were received from customers; enter the receipts on the accounts system.

Date	Receipt type	Customer	Amount	Details
19 July	Cheque No. 542321	J Hollingham	2849.37	Payment for invoice 1001 including credit note CR34
12 July	Cheque No. 222547	Kerry Jenkins	758.34	Payment for invoice 0093
13 July	BACS	Harry Bucket	2767.34	Payment for invoice 1003

TASK 8

The following cheque payments were sent to suppliers; enter the payments on the accounts system and **raise the relevant remittance advices.**

Date	Cheque No:	Supplier	Amount	Details
14th July	170012	Radcliff & Sons	5362.14	Payment for invoice 1874
17th July	170013	Tennison Bros	2801.00	Payment for invoice B-321

TASK 9

Enter the Petty cash payments into the computer

Petty Cash Voucher	
Date:	10.07.XX
Voucher No:	152
Details	£
Stationery (no Vat)	19.90
Authorised By;	*Nina Birk*
Receipt attached	

Petty Cash Voucher	
Date:	20.07.XX
Voucher No:	187
Details	£
Postage	343.55
VAT	68.71
Total	412.26
Authorised By;	*Nina Birk*
Receipt attached	

TASK 10

Refer to the following cash sales and enter receipts into the bank current account on the computer.

Date	Receipt ref	Gross	VAT	NET	Nominal code
13 July	REC101	1,200.00	200.00	1,000.00	4000
15 July	REC102	2,879.40	479.90	2,399.50	4001
15 July	REC103	1,194.90	199.15	995.75	4000

TASK 11

Print out the following reports:

> Trial Balance Report
>
> Sales Day Book
>
> Purchase Day Book
>
> Customer Activity Report
>
> Supplier Activity Report
>
> Aged Creditors Report
>
> Aged Debtors Report
>
> Print Statement for Paul McCallum

TASK 12

Enter the following journal

<table>
<tr><td colspan="4" align="center">**Ref : JNL004**</td></tr>
<tr><td>**Date**</td><td>**Account Name & Code**</td><td>**Dr**</td><td>**Cr**</td></tr>
<tr><td>25.07.XX</td><td>Drawings</td><td>3,441.00</td><td></td></tr>
<tr><td></td><td>Bank</td><td></td><td>3,441.00</td></tr>
<tr><td colspan="4">Being the transfer of cash for personal use.</td></tr>
</table>

TASK 13

Refer to the following email below from Nina Birk and **save a screenshot of your work** and save with a **suitable file name**.

<table>
<tr><td colspan="2" align="center">**E-Mail**</td></tr>
<tr><td colspan="2">From: Nina Birk
Date: 19th July 20XX
Subject: Customer change of address</td></tr>
<tr><td colspan="2">Hello
A credit customer Harry Bucket has moved premises. New address as follows:
137 Chester Road
Capel Corner
CR3 2SA
Telephone: 08459 754 256
Please ensure that this is updated on the computerised accounts system.
Thanks
Nina</td></tr>
</table>

TASK 14

The following cheque payments were sent to suppliers; enter the payments on the accounts system.

Date	A/c No	Supplier	Cheque No	Details	Amount
28 July	PL03	Skipton & Co	170014	Invoice 1087	501.00
28 July	PL01	Radcliff & Sons	170015	Invoice 1099	660.00

TASK 15

The following payments were received from customers; enter the receipts on the accounts system.

Date	Customer	Cheque No	Details	Amount (£)
28 July	J Hollingham	087651	Invoice 1052	2675.52
28 July	Harry Bucket	198871	Invoice 1054	Part Payment of 500.00

TASK 16

On 14th July a member of staff buys a Tennis Racquet paying you £50.00 in Cash. This is inclusive of sales tax. Enter this in to the bank current account and use reference ST5 for the transaction.

TASK 17

On 19th July, you sold a 'Golf Club' to a customer and they paid £45.00 (Plus VAT) debit card. Use reference CS03.

TASK 18

A cheque you received from Kerry Jenkins for £758.34 (Cheque No 222547) has been returned by the bank marked 'Refer to Drawer – Insufficient Funds'. Process this returned cheque through the records, dated 12th July.

TASK 19

You are asked to set up a monthly standing order for Insurance for £100.00 (Exempt VAT) for a period of 12 months commencing on 28th July. There is no VAT on this transaction. The Insurance is payable to Ipswich Union. **Take a screenshot** of the details and save as a 'Word' document with a suitable file name. Process July's payment.

TASK 20

Refer to the following email below from Nina Birk

E-Mail
From: Nina Birk
Date: 31st July 20XX
Subject: Customer write off
Hello In view of Paul McCallum, we have continuously chased this customer for payment and received no response. I have decided that we should write off the balance of their account at 31st July. Please ensure that this is done. Thanks Nina

TASK 21

You are given the following bank statement and are asked to produce a bank reconciliation at 31st July, processing any adjustments that may be necessary.

Sully Bank plc
201 Main Road
Gillingham
Kent
ME3 5TF

Sports Gear
34 Hockey Avenue
Tennison
London
EC1V 1NY

31st July 20XX
Statement no: 1001

Account number 00678432

Statement of Account

Date: July 2011	Details	Paid out £	Paid in £	Balance £
01 July	Opening balance			3325.40C
12 July	Counter Credit		758.34	4083.74C
12 July	Dishonoured cheque	758.34		3325.40C
13 July	BACS		2767.34	6092.74C
13 July	Counter credit		1200.00	7292.74C
14 July	Counter credit		50.00	7342.74C
15 July	Counter credit		2879.40	10222.14C
15 July	Counter credit		1194.90	11417.04C
19 July	Cheque 170013	2801.00		8616.04C
20 July	Counter Credit		2849.37	11465.41C
20 July	Debit Card		54.00	11519.41C
25 July	Counter Debit	3441.00		8078.41C
29 July	Counter Credit		2675.52	10753.93C
29 July	Counter Credit		500.00	11253.93C
29 July	Standing Order – Ipswich Union	100.00		11153.93C
31 July	Bank charges	32.19		11121.74C
	D = Debit C = Credit			

TASK 22

Transfer £432.16 from the bank current account to the petty cash account. Use reference TRF01 for this transaction and date it 31st July.

TASK 23

Print the following reports

- Customer Address List
- Customer Activity (detailed report)
- Supplier Activity (detailed report)
- Period Trial Balance for the month of July (inc. opening balances)
- Nominal Ledger Activity Report for the following accounts
  - Bank Current Account
  - Petty Cash Account

PRACTICE PAPER 5

WAY TO WORK

THE SITUATION

This assignment is based on an existing business, Way to Work.

At the start of the business they operated under a manual bookkeeping system but they have now decided that from 1st March 20XX the accounting system will become computerised.

Some nominal ledger accounts have already been allocated suitable account codes. **You may need to amend or create other account codes.**

Way to Work's financial year starts in March.

Their company details are:-

Way to Work

55 Upper Street

London

N1 9PE

You are employed as an accounting technician.

The business is registered for VAT. The company's products are standard rated for VAT (20%).

Set the company's financial year to start in March 20XX

TASK 1

Refer to the customer listing below and set up customer records to open Sales Ledger accounts for each customer.

Customer account code	Customer name, address and contact details	Customer account details
JP01	Morgan, Smith & Winston City Road Islington London N1 9PL	Credit limit: £7000 Payment Terms: 30 days Opening Balance: £1172.34 (relates to invoice INV021 dated 14th February 20XX)
JP02	Cyril West Grays West Grays Inn Road London WC1 1LT	Credit limit: £8500 Payment Terms: 30 days Opening Balance: £2954.00 (relates to invoice INV045 dated 22nd February 20XX).
JP03	Wallace & Gromit Ltd 134 Upper Street Islington London N1 2PT	Credit limit: £17000 Payment Terms: 30 days Opening Balance: £3180.00 (relates to invoice INV033 dated 18th February 20XX)
JP04	Star Paper 66 White Lion Street London N1 5RX	Credit limit: £12500 Payment Terms: 30 days Opening Balance: £1867.34 – relates to invoice INV034 dated 22nd February 20XX)

TASK 2

Refer to the supplier listing below and set up supplier records to open Purchase Ledger accounts for each supplier.

Supplier account code	Supplier name, address and contact details	Supplier account details
SP01	Paper Products UK South Down Trading Estate Sheffield S15 4DR	Credit limit: £8500 Payment Terms: 30 days Opening Balance: £445.23 – relates to invoice 0165 dated 28th February 20XX).
SP02	Wallace & Gromit Ltd 134 Upper Street Islington London N1 2PT	Credit limit: £12000 Payment Terms: 30 days Opening Balance: £6711.00 (relates to invoice 02183 dated 11th February 20XX)
SP03	Whole Office Furniture 176 East Way Leeds LD4 6PP	Credit limit: £4000 Payment Terms: 30 days Opening Balance: £1875.21 (relates to invoice 1028 dated 26th February 20XX)
SP04	Stationery World 32 Great Portland Road London WC1V 6HH	Credit limit: £16500 Payment Terms: 30 days Opening Balance: £9504.32 (relates to invoice 0187 dated 18th February 20XX).

TASK 3.1

Refer to the list of General ledger balances below. Enter the opening balances into the computer, making sure you select the appropriate general ledger account codes.

List of general ledger balances as at 01.03.20XX

Account name	£	£
Motor Vehicle	14000.00	
Furniture and Fixtures	8000.00	
Bank	6210.81	
Petty Cash	100.00	
Sales Ledger Control Account *	9173.68	
Purchase Ledger Control Account*		18535.76
Capital		34000.00
Drawings	1000.00	
Stationery Sales		903.73
CD Roms Sales		855.00
Printer Accessories Sales		9842.00
Stationery purchases	2400.00	
CD Rom purchases	210.00	
Printer Accessory purchases	15000.00	
Wages and Salaries	5600.00	
General Expenses	342.00	
Rent	2100.00	
Note You do not need to enter these figures as you have already entered opening balances for customers and suppliers.		

TASK 3.2

Transfer £1500.00 from the bank current account to the bank deposit account. Date the transaction 1st March and use reference TRANS01.

TASK 3.3

Print out the following reports and **identify and correct any errors**.

- Customer Address List
- Supplier Address List
- Trial Balance

TASK 4

Enter the sales invoices onto the computer.

Date	A/C No.	Invoice Ref	Description	Nominal Code	Gross £	VAT £	Net £
3 Mar	JP02	INV041	Stationery	4000	936.00	156.00	780.00
3 Mar	JP04	INV042	CD Roms	4001	1105.20	184.20	921.00
5 Mar	JP01	INV043	Printer Accessory	4002	5251.20	875.20	4376.00
7 Mar	JP03	INV044	Printer Accessory	4002	549.60	91.60	458.00
7 Mar	JP01	INV045	Stationery	4000	7452.00	1242.00	6210.00

TASK 5

On 17th March you send a credit note (CR51) to Star Paper (Account No JP04) for Printer Accessories.

The total is £251.27 plus tax.

TASK 6

Enter the purchases invoices into the computer.

Date	A/C No.	Invoice Ref	Description	Nominal Code	Gross	Vat	Net
10 Mar	SP01	0200	Stationery	5000	586.80	97.80	489.00
11 Mar	SP02	02241	CD Roms	5001	414.00	69.00	345.00
11 Mar	SP03	1098	Printer Accessory	5002	9153.60	1525.60	7628.00
14 Mar	SP04	0197	Stationery	5000	4280.40	713.40	3567.00

TASK 7

Enter the following purchase credit note onto the computer system.

Date	A/C No	Supplier	N/C	Credit Note Ref	Amount	Details
19 Mar	SP04	Stationery World	5000	RF287	124.08	Plus Tax

TASK 8

The following payments were received from customers; enter the receipts on the accounts system.

Date	Cheque Number	Customer	Amount	Details
15 Mar	203998	Morgan, Smith & Winston	1172.34	Payment for invoice INV021
17 Mar	103112	Cyril West	2954.00	Payment for invoice INV045
19 Mar	011211	Star Paper	1565.82	Payment for invoice INV034 including credit note CR51

TASK 9

The following cheque payments were sent to suppliers; enter the payments on the accounts system dated 31st March, and **raise the relevant remittance advices**.

Supplier	Cheque No:	Amount	Details
Paper Products UK	100076	445.23	Payment for invoice 0165
Whole Office Furniture	100077	1875.21	Payment for invoice 1028
Stationery World	100078	9504.32	Payment for invoice 0187

TASK 10

On 15th March you transfer £600.00 from the Bank account to the Petty Cash account. Use reference TRANS02 for this transaction.

TASK 11

Enter the following petty cash payments into the computer:

Date	Ref	Nominal Code	Details	Net	VAT	Gross
19 Mar	056	7200	Electricity	84.10	16.82	100.92
20 Mar	057	6201	Advertising	327.00	65.40	392.40

TASK 12

On the 28th March, a member of staff purchases a 'Printer Accessories' from you and pays you a total of £123.48 in cash. This is inclusive of VAT of £20.58. Use reference ST4 for this transaction and enter the funds in to the bank current account.

TASK 13

A cheque sent to Paper Products for £445.23 (cheque number 100076) has not been delivered to the supplier. Cancel this cheque through the records dated 31st March 20XX.

TASK 14

On the 31st March you are asked to set up a monthly standing order for Rent for £568.00 (Exempt VAT) for a period of 12 months commencing on 31st March. The Rent is payable to ICPW Bank. Process the payment for March.

TASK 15

You are given the following bank statement and are asked to produce a bank reconciliation at 31st March, processing any adjustments that may be necessary.

Islington Bank Plc	
201 Upper Street	
Islington	
London	
N1 9PE	

Way to Work
55 Upper Street
London
N1 9PE

31st March 20XX
Statement no: 0002

Account number: 32543211

Statement of Account

Date: March 20XX	Details	Paid out £	Paid in £	Balance £
01 Mar	Opening balance			6210.81C
01 Mar	Transfer	1500.00		4710.81C
15 Mar	Transfer	600.00		4110.81C
18 Mar	Counter Credit		1172.34	5283.15C
18 Mar	Counter Credit		2954.00	8237.15C
19 Mar	Counter Credit		1565.82	9802.97C
23 Mar	Cancelled cheque		445.23	10248.20C
26 Mar	100017	1875.21		8372.99C
28 Mar	Counter credit		123.48	8496.47C
31 Mar	100076	445.23		8051.24C
31 Mar	Standing Order – ICPW Bank	568.00		7483.24C
31 Mar	Bank Charges	123.45		7359.79C
	D = Debit C = Credit			

TASK 16

Print the following reports

- Customer Activity (detailed report)
- Supplier Activity (detailed report)
- Trial Balance for the month of March
- Audit Trial for March only (inc opening balances)
- Nominal Ledger Activity Report for the following accounts
  - Bank Current Account
  - Petty Cash Account

Section 2

ANSWERS TO PRACTICE QUESTIONS

PRACTICE PAPER 1

TOY SHOP ANSWERS

TASK 3.3

Customer Address List

Toy Shop

Customer Address List

Address Types: All

Customer Name	Address	Contact name	Phone	Mobile	Email	Fax
Busy Bee Toys (BB01)	832 High Street Oxford OX2 3WG United Kingdom	Main Contact				
Forming Fun (FF02)	21 Newton Quay Knott Mill Manchester M6 3RJ United Kingdom	Main Contact				
Space Models (SM03)	13 Central Street Perth Scotland United Kingdom	Main Contact				
Teddy T's Party (TP04)	3 Paradise Street Wokingham WO4 6QP United Kingdom	Main Contact				

TASK 3.3

Supplier Address List

Toy Shop

Supplier Address List

Address Types: All

Supplier Name	Address	Contact name	Phone	Mobile	Email	Fax
Abacus C & C (PL01)	Unit 31 Kitts Industrial Estate St Helens Lancs United Kingdom	Main Contact				
Compugames Ltd (PL02)	6 Jury Road Dublin Eire United Kingdom	Main Contact				
Space Models (PL03)	13 Central Street Perth Scotland SC4 8RQ United Kingdom	Main Contact				
Toys Unlimited (PL04)	95 Cusaden Road Edinburgh Scotland United Kingdom	Main Contact				

TASK 3.3

Period Trial Balance Report

Toy Shop

Trial Balance Report

From Date: 30/04/2015   To Date: 31/05/2015

Nominal Code	Name	Debits	Credits
0040	Furniture and fixtures - Cost	5,800.00	
0050	Motor Vehicles - Cost	3,000.00	
1100	Trade Debtors	2,223.60	
1200	Current	3,725.00	
1210	Petty Cash	300.00	
1220	Deposit	500.00	
2100	Trade Creditors		2,157.60
2200	VAT on Sales		543.00
2201	VAT on Purchases	109.00	
3000	Capital		20,000.00
3260	Drawings	355.00	
4000	Sales - Computer Games		6,080.00
4001	Sales - Jigsaws		700.00
4002	Sales - Boxed Games		1,967.00
5000	Purchases - Computer Games	8,000.00	
5001	Purchases - Jigsaws	3,200.00	
5002	Purchases - Boxed Games	2,465.00	
7100	Rent and Rates	1,550.00	
7200	Electricity	167.00	
7500	Office Stationery	53.00	
	TOTAL	£31,447.60	£31,447.60

TASK 7

Abacus C & C – remittance advice

Toy Shop

Toy Shop
64 Long Lane Langhorne North Yorkshire YO21 3EJ

Telephone: VAT Number
07711 290287   123456780

Abacus C & C (PL01)

Unit 31, Kitts Industrial Estate, St Helens, Lancs, United Kingdom

Remittance Advice

Reference: Chq No. 101333   Date Paid: 22/05/2015   Amount Paid: 369.60

Ref	Number	Date	Total Amount	Amount Paid
B/1874		30/04/2015	369.60	369.60
			Total Paid:	369.60

Compugames – remittance advice

Toy Shop

Toy Shop
64 Long Lane Langhorne North Yorkshire YO21 3EJ

Telephone: VAT Number
07711 290287   123456780

Compugames Ltd (PL02)

6 Jury Road, Dublin, Eire, United Kingdom

Remittance Advice

Reference: Chq No. 101334   Date Paid: 22/05/2015   Amount Paid: 1,005.60

Ref	Number	Date	Total Amount	Amount Paid
1087		30/04/2015	511.20	511.20
145215		05/05/2015	600.00	600.00
11245		15/05/2015	-105.60	-105.60
			Total Paid:	1,005.60

TASK 11

Trial Balance Report

From Date: 30/04/2015   To Date: 31/05/2015

Nominal Code	Name	Debits	Credits
0040	Furniture and fixtures - Cost	5,800.00	
0050	Motor Vehicles - Cost	3,000.00	
1100	Trade Debtors	10,897.20	
1200	Current	6,068.60	
1210	Petty Cash	255.52	
1220	Deposit	500.00	
2100	Trade Creditors		3,034.80
2200	VAT on Sales		2,775.90
2201	VAT on Purchases	483.48	
3000	Capital		20,000.00
3260	Drawings	2,355.00	
4000	Sales - Computer Games		15,340.00
4001	Sales - Jigsaws		3,099.50
4002	Sales - Boxed Games		2,467.00
5000	Purchases - Computer Games	9,362.00	
5001	Purchases - Jigsaws	3,218.00	
5002	Purchases - Boxed Games	2,965.00	
7100	Rent and Rates	1,550.00	
7200	Electricity	167.00	
7500	Office Stationery	53.00	
8201	Subscriptions	32.00	
8205	Refreshments	10.40	
	TOTAL	£46,717.20	£46,717.20

TASK 11

Sales Day Book

Toy Shop

Sales Day Book Report

From Date: 30/04/2015

To Date: 31/05/2015

Type: Sales QE Invoice

Trans ID	Type	Date	Name	Invoice Number	Ref	Details	Net	VAT	Total
14	Sales QE Invoice	04/05/2015	Busy Bee Toys		2021		2,585.00	517.00	3,102.00
15	Sales QE Invoice	04/05/2015	Forming Fun		2022		500.00	100.00	600.00
16	Sales QE Invoice	06/05/2015	Teddy T's Party		2023		5,000.00	1,000.00	6,000.00
						TOTAL	£8,085.00	£1,617.00	£9,702.00

TASK 11

Sales Return Day Book

Toy Shop

Sales Day Book Report

From Date: 30/04/2015

To Date: 31/05/2015

Type: Sales QE Credit

Trans ID	Type	Date	Name	Invoice Number	Ref	Details	Net	VAT	Total
17	Sales QE Credit	13/05/2015	Teddy T's Party		CN101	Return faulty comp. games	-320.00	-64.00	-384.00
						TOTAL	-£320.00	-£64.00	-£384.00

TASK 11

Purchase Day Book

Toy Shop

Purchase Day Book Report

From Date: 30/04/2015

To Date: 31/05/2015

Type: Purchase QE Invoice

Trans ID	Type	Date	Name	Invoice Number	Ref	Details	Net	VAT	Total
18	Purchase QE Invoice	03/05/2015	Abacus C & C		B/989		450.00	90.00	540.00
19	Purchase QE Invoice	05/05/2015	Compugames Ltd		145215		500.00	100.00	600.00
20	Purchase QE Invoice	10/05/2015	Space Models		C-32632		1,000.00	200.00	1,200.00
21	Purchase QE Invoice	10/05/2015	Toys Unlimited		12421		18.00	0.00	18.00
						TOTAL	£1,968.00	£390.00	£2,358.00

TASK 11

Customer Activity Report

Toy Shop

Customer Activity Report

From Date: 30/04/2015

To Date: 31/05/2015

Busy Bee Toys (BB01)

Date	Number	Reference	Type	Net	VAT	Total	Discount	Outstanding
30/04/2015		021	Customer OB Invoice	349.20	0.00	349.20		0.00
04/05/2015		2021	Sales QE Invoice	2,585.00	517.00	3,102.00		3,102.00
17/05/2015		Chq No. 100322	Customer Receipt			-349.20	0.00	0.00
						3,102.00		3,102.00

Forming Fun (FF02)

Date	Number	Reference	Type	Net	VAT	Total	Discount	Outstanding
30/04/2015		035	Customer OB Invoice	99.60	0.00	99.60		0.00
04/05/2015		2022	Sales QE Invoice	500.00	100.00	600.00		600.00
17/05/2015		Chq No. 267543	Customer Receipt			-99.60	0.00	0.00
						600.00		600.00

Space Models (SM03)

Date	Number	Reference	Type	Net	VAT	Total	Discount	Outstanding
30/04/2015		093	Customer OB Invoice	1,195.20	0.00	1,195.20		1,195.20
						1,195.20		1,195.20

Teddy T's Party (TP04)

Date	Number	Reference	Type	Net	VAT	Total	Discount	Outstanding
30/04/2015		1003	Customer OB Invoice	579.60	0.00	579.60		0.00
06/05/2015		2023	Sales QE Invoice	5,000.00	1,000.00	6,000.00		6,000.00
13/05/2015		CN101	Sales QE Credit	-320.00	-64.00	-384.00		0.00
26/05/2015		BACS	Customer Receipt			-195.60	0.00	0.00
						6,000.00		6,000.00

TASK 11

Supplier Activity Report

Toy Shop

Supplier Activity Report

From Date: 30/04/2015

To Date: 31/05/2015

Abacus C & C (PL01)

Date	Number	Reference	Type	Net	VAT	Total	Discount	Outstanding
30/04/2015		B/1874	Supplier OB Invoice	369.60	0.00	369.60		0.00
03/05/2015		B/989	Purchase QE Invoice	450.00	90.00	540.00		540.00
22/05/2015		Chq No. 101333	Supplier Payment			-369.60	0.00	0.00
						540.00		**540.00**

Compugames Ltd (PL02)

Date	Number	Reference	Type	Net	VAT	Total	Discount	Outstanding
30/04/2015		1087	Supplier OB Invoice	511.20	0.00	511.20		0.00
05/05/2015		145215	Purchase QE Invoice	500.00	100.00	600.00		0.00
15/05/2015		11245	Purchase QE Credit	-88.00	-17.60	-105.60		0.00
22/05/2015		Chq No. 101334	Supplier Payment			-1,005.60	0.00	0.00
						0.00		**0.00**

Space Models (PL03)

Date	Number	Reference	Type	Net	VAT	Total	Discount	Outstanding
30/04/2015		F-0193	Supplier OB Invoice	306.00	0.00	306.00		306.00
10/05/2015		C-32632	Purchase QE Invoice	1,000.00	200.00	1,200.00		1,200.00
						1,506.00		**1,506.00**

Toys Unlimited (PL04)

Date	Number	Reference	Type	Net	VAT	Total	Discount	Outstanding
30/04/2015		W/032	Supplier OB Invoice	970.80	0.00	970.80		970.80
10/05/2015		12421	Purchase QE Invoice	18.00	0.00	18.00		18.00
						988.80		**988.80**

TASK 11

Aged Creditors Report

Toy Shop

Aged Creditors Breakdown

To Date: 31/05/2015

Supplier	Date	Reference	Total	O/S Amt	< 30 days	< 60 days	< 90 days	< 120 days	Older
Abacus C & C (PL01) Credit limit: £5,500.00 Terms: 30 days									
	03/05/2015	B/989	540.00	540.00	540.00				
			£540.00	£540.00	£0.00	£0.00	£0.00	£0.00	
Space Models (PL03) Credit limit: £2,000.00 Terms: 30 days									
	10/05/2015	C-32632	1,200.00	1,200.00	1,200.00				
	30/04/2015	F-0193	306.00	306.00		306.00			
			£1,506.00	£1,200.00	£306.00	£0.00	£0.00	£0.00	
Toys Unlimited (PL04) Credit limit: £2,000.00 Terms: 30 days									
	10/05/2015	12421	18.00	18.00	18.00				
	30/04/2015	W/032	970.80	970.80		970.80			
			£988.80	£18.00	£970.80	£0.00	£0.00	£0.00	
		TOTAL	£3,034.80	£1,758.00	£1,276.80	£0.00	£0.00	£0.00	

TASK 11

Aged Debtors Report

Toy Shop

Aged Debtors Breakdown

To Date: 31/05/2015

Customer	Date	Reference	Total	O/S Amt	< 30 days	< 60 days	< 90 days	< 120 days	Older
Busy Bee Toys (BB01) Credit limit: £4,000.00 Terms: 30 days									
	04/05/2015	QE-2021	3,102.00	3,102.00	3,102.00				
				£3,102.00	£3,102.00	£0.00	£0.00	£0.00	£0.00
Forming Fun (FF02) Credit limit: £4,000.00 Terms: 30 days									
	04/05/2015	QE-2022	600.00	600.00	600.00				
				£600.00	£600.00	£0.00	£0.00	£0.00	£0.00
Space Models (SM03) Credit limit: £3,000.00 Terms: 30 days									
	30/04/2015	OB-093	1,195.20	1,195.20		1,195.20			
				£1,195.20	£0.00	£1,195.20	£0.00	£0.00	£0.00
Teddy T's Party (TP04) Credit limit: £7,000.00 Terms: 30 days									
	06/05/2015	QE-2023	6,000.00	6,000.00	6,000.00				
				£6,000.00	£6,000.00	£0.00	£0.00	£0.00	£0.00
			TOTAL	£10,897.20	£9,702.00	£1,195.20	£0.00	£0.00	£0.00

TASK 12

Customer address screen shot

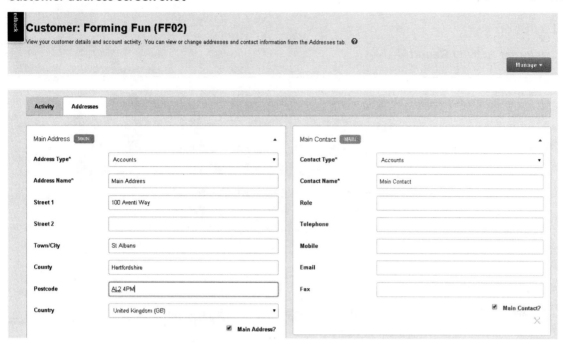

TASK 23

Customer Activity (detailed) Report

Toy Shop

Customer Activity Report

From Date: 30/04/2015

To Date: 31/05/2015

Busy Bee Toys (BB01)

Date	Number	Reference	Type	Net	VAT	Total	Discount	Outstanding
30/04/2015		021	Customer OB Invoice	349.20	0.00	349.20		0.00
04/05/2015		2021	Sales QE Invoice	2,585.00	517.00	3,102.00		0.00
17/05/2015		Chq No. 100322	Customer Receipt			-349.20	0.00	0.00
29/05/2015		Chq No. 104662	Customer Receipt			-3,102.00	0.00	0.00
						0.00		0.00

Forming Fun (FF02)

Date	Number	Reference	Type	Net	VAT	Total	Discount	Outstanding
30/04/2015		035	Customer OB Invoice	99.60	0.00	99.60		99.60
04/05/2015		2022	Sales QE Invoice	500.00	100.00	600.00		200.00
17/05/2015		Chq No. 267543	Customer Receipt			-99.60		0.00
17/05/2015		Bounced Cheque	Customer Refund			99.60		0.00
29/05/2015		Chq No. 828100	Customer Receipt			-400.00	0.00	0.00
						299.60		299.60

Space Models (SM03)

Date	Number	Reference	Type	Net	VAT	Total	Discount	Outstanding
30/04/2015		093	Customer OB Invoice	1,195.20	0.00	1,195.20		1,195.20
						1,195.20		1,195.20

Teddy T's Party (TP04)

Date	Number	Reference	Type	Net	VAT	Total	Discount	Outstanding
30/04/2015		1003	Customer OB Invoice	579.60	0.00	579.60		0.00
06/05/2015		2023	Sales QE Invoice	5,000.00	1,000.00	6,000.00		0.00
13/05/2015		CN101	Sales QE Credit	-320.00	-64.00	-384.00		0.00
26/05/2015		BACS	Customer Receipt			-195.60	0.00	0.00
29/05/2015		Chq No. 672522	Customer Receipt			-6,000.00	0.00	0.00
						0.00		0.00

TASK 23

Supplier Activity (detailed) Report

Toy Shop

Supplier Activity Report

From Date: 30/04/2015

To Date: 31/05/2015

Abacus C & C (PL01)

Date	Number	Reference	Type	Net	VAT	Total	Discount	Outstanding
30/04/2015		B/1874	Supplier OB Invoice	369.60	0.00	369.60		0.00
03/05/2015		B/989	Purchase QE Invoice	450.00	90.00	540.00		0.00
22/05/2015		Chq No. 101333	Supplier Payment			-369.60	0.00	0.00
28/05/2015		BACS	Supplier Payment			-540.00	0.00	0.00
						0.00		0.00

Compugames Ltd (PL02)

Date	Number	Reference	Type	Net	VAT	Total	Discount	Outstanding
30/04/2015		1087	Supplier OB Invoice	511.20	0.00	511.20		0.00
05/05/2015		145215	Purchase QE Invoice	500.00	100.00	600.00		0.00
15/05/2015		11245	Purchase QE Credit	-88.00	-17.60	-105.60		0.00
22/05/2015		Chq No. 101334	Supplier Payment			-1,005.60	0.00	0.00
						0.00		0.00

Space Models (PL03)

Date	Number	Reference	Type	Net	VAT	Total	Discount	Outstanding
30/04/2015		F-0193	Supplier OB Invoice	306.00	0.00	306.00		0.00
10/05/2015		C-32632	Purchase QE Invoice	1,000.00	200.00	1,200.00		1,200.00
28/05/2015		Chq No. 101335	Supplier Payment			-306.00	0.00	0.00
						1,200.00		1,200.00

Toys Unlimited (PL04)

Date	Number	Reference	Type	Net	VAT	Total	Discount	Outstanding
30/04/2015		W/032	Supplier OB Invoice	970.80	0.00	970.80		520.80
10/05/2015		12421	Purchase QE Invoice	18.00	0.00	18.00		18.00
28/05/2015		Chq No. 101336	Supplier Payment			-450.00	0.00	0.00
						538.80		538.80

TASK 23

Period Trial Balance for May

Toy Shop

Trial Balance Report

From Date: 30/04/2015   To Date: 31/05/2015

Nominal Code	Name	Debits	Credits
0040	Furniture and fixtures - Cost	5,800.00	
0050	Motor Vehicles - Cost	3,000.00	
1100	Trade Debtors	1,494.80	
1200	Current	24,238.20	
1210	Petty Cash	300.00	
1220	Deposit	500.00	
2100	Trade Creditors		1,738.80
2200	VAT on Sales		2,819.90
2201	VAT on Purchases	483.48	
2500	Loan Account		10,000.00
3000	Capital		20,000.00
3260	Drawings	2,355.00	
4000	Sales - Computer Games		15,560.00
4001	Sales - Jigsaws		3,099.50
4002	Sales - Boxed Games		2,467.00
4900	Other Income		45.00
5000	Purchases - Computer Games	9,362.00	
5001	Purchases - Jigsaws	3,218.00	
5002	Purchases - Boxed Games	2,965.00	
7100	Rent and Rates	1,048.00	
7200	Electricity	669.00	
7500	Office Stationery	53.00	
7610	Insurance	100.00	
7900	Bank charges and interest	101.32	
8201	Subscriptions	32.00	
8205	Refreshments	10.40	
	TOTAL	**£55,730.20**	**£55,730.20**

TASK 23

Audit Trail for May (detailed – transactions only including bank reconciled)

Toy Shop

Audit Trail Breakdown

From Date: 30/04/2015

To Date: 31/05/2015

Type: All

Trans ID	Entry Date	Created By	Trans Date	Name	Type	Invoice Number	Ref	Ledger Account	Debit	Credit	Bank Reconciled	Deleted
1	30/05/2015	Sally Brummitt	30/04/2015	Busy Bee Toys (BB01)	Customer OB Invoice		021	Opening Balances Control Account (9998)	0.00	349.20	No	No
1	30/05/2015	Sally Brummitt	30/04/2015	Busy Bee Toys (BB01)	Customer OB Invoice		021	Trade Debtors (1100)	349.20	0.00	No	No
2	30/05/2015	Sally Brummitt	30/04/2015	Forming Fun (FF02)	Customer OB Invoice		035	Opening Balances Control Account (9998)	0.00	99.60	No	No
2	30/05/2015	Sally Brummitt	30/04/2015	Forming Fun (FF02)	Customer OB Invoice		035	Trade Debtors (1100)	99.60	0.00	No	No
3	30/05/2015	Sally Brummitt	30/04/2015	Space Models (SM03)	Customer OB Invoice		093	Opening Balances Control Account (9998)	0.00	1,195.20	No	No
3	30/05/2015	Sally Brummitt	30/04/2015	Space Models (SM03)	Customer OB Invoice		093	Trade Debtors (1100)	1,195.20	0.00	No	No

Trans ID	Entry Date	Created By	Trans Date	Name	Type	Invoice Number	Ref	Ledger Account	Debit	Credit	Bank Reconciled	Deleted
4	30/05/2015	Sally Brummitt	30/04/2015	Teddy T's Party (TP04)	Customer OB Invoice		1003	Opening Balances Control Account (9998)	0.00	579.60	No	No
4	30/05/2015	Sally Brummitt	30/04/2015	Teddy T's Party (TP04)	Customer OB Invoice		1003	Trade Debtors (1100)	579.60	0.00	No	No
5	30/05/2015	Sally Brummitt	30/04/2015	Abacus C & C (PL01)	Supplier OB Invoice		B/1874	Opening Balances Control Account (9998)	369.60	0.00	No	No
5	30/05/2015	Sally Brummitt	30/04/2015	Abacus C & C (PL01)	Supplier OB Invoice		B/1874	Trade Creditors (2100)	0.00	369.60	No	No
6	30/05/2015	Sally Brummitt	30/04/2015	Compugames Ltd (PL02)	Supplier OB Invoice		1087	Opening Balances Control Account (9998)	511.20	0.00	No	No
6	30/05/2015	Sally Brummitt	30/04/2015	Compugames Ltd (PL02)	Supplier OB Invoice		1087	Trade Creditors (2100)	0.00	511.20	No	No
7	30/05/2015	Sally Brummitt	30/04/2015	Space Models (PL03)	Supplier OB Invoice		F-0193	Opening Balances Control Account (9998)	306.00	0.00	No	No
7	30/05/2015	Sally Brummitt	30/04/2015	Space Models (PL03)	Supplier OB Invoice		F-0193	Trade Creditors (2100)	0.00	306.00	No	No
8	30/05/2015	Sally Brummitt	30/04/2015	Toys Unlimited (PL04)	Supplier OB Invoice		W/032	Opening Balances Control Account (9998)	970.80	0.00	No	No
8	30/05/2015	Sally Brummitt	30/04/2015	Toys Unlimited (PL04)	Supplier OB Invoice		W/032	Trade Creditors (2100)	0.00	970.80	No	No
9	30/05/2015	Sally Brummitt	30/04/2015		Bank Opening Balance			Opening Balances Control Account (9998)	0.00	4,225.00	No	No

No	Date	Name	Date	Type	Ref	Account	Debit	Credit		
9	30/05/2015	Sally Brummitt	30/04/2015	Bank Opening Balance		Current (1200)	4,225.00	0.00	Yes	No
10	30/05/2015	Sally Brummitt	30/04/2015	Bank Opening Balance		Opening Balances Control Account (9998)	0.00	300.00	No	No
10	30/05/2015	Sally Brummitt	30/04/2015	Bank Opening Balance		Petty Cash (1210)	300.00	0.00	No	No
11	30/05/2015	Sally Brummitt	30/04/2015	Journal Opening Balance	O/Bals as at 01/05/15	Motor Vehicles - Cost (0050)	3,000.00	0.00	No	Yes
11	30/05/2015	Sally Brummitt	30/04/2015	Journal Opening Balance	O/Bals as at 01/05/15	Opening Balances Control Account (9998)	0.00	3,000.00	No	Yes
11	30/05/2015	Sally Brummitt	30/04/2015	Journal Opening Balance	O/Bals as at 01/05/15	Motor Vehicles - Cost (0050)	0.00	3,000.00	No	Yes
11	30/05/2015	Sally Brummitt	30/04/2015	Journal Opening Balance	O/Bals as at 01/05/15	Opening Balances Control Account (9998)	3,000.00	0.00	No	Yes
12	30/05/2015	Sally Brummitt	30/04/2015	Journal Opening Balance	O/Bals as at 01/05/15	Motor Vehicles - Cost (0050)	3,000.00	0.00	No	No
12	30/05/2015	Sally Brummitt	30/04/2015	Journal Opening Balance	O/Bals as at 01/05/15	Furniture and fixtures - Cost (0040)	5,800.00	0.00	No	No
12	30/05/2015	Sally Brummitt	30/04/2015	Journal Opening Balance	O/Bals as at 01/05/15	Opening Balances Control Account (9998)	543.00	0.00	No	No
12	30/05/2015	Sally Brummitt	30/04/2015	Journal Opening Balance	O/Bals as at 01/05/15	VAT on Purchases (2201)	109.00	0.00	No	No
12	30/05/2015	Sally Brummitt	30/04/2015	Journal Opening Balance	O/Bals as at 01/05/15	Opening Balances Control Account (9998)	20,000.00	0.00	No	No

No	Date	Name	Date	Type	Ref	Account	Debit	Credit		
12	30/05/2015	Sally Brummitt	30/04/2015	Journal Opening Balance	O/Bals as at 01/05/15	Drawings (3260)	355.00	0.00	No	No
12	30/05/2015	Sally Brummitt	30/04/2015	Journal Opening Balance	O/Bals as at 01/05/15	Opening Balances Control Account (9998)	6,080.00	0.00	No	No
12	30/05/2015	Sally Brummitt	30/04/2015	Journal Opening Balance	O/Bals as at 01/05/15	Opening Balances Control Account (9998)	700.00	0.00	No	No
12	30/05/2015	Sally Brummitt	30/04/2015	Journal Opening Balance	O/Bals as at 01/05/15	Opening Balances Control Account (9998)	1,967.00	0.00	No	No
12	30/05/2015	Sally Brummitt	30/04/2015	Journal Opening Balance	O/Bals as at 01/05/15	Purchases - Computer Games (5000)	8,000.00	0.00	No	No
12	30/05/2015	Sally Brummitt	30/04/2015	Journal Opening Balance	O/Bals as at 01/05/15	Purchases - Jigsaws (5001)	3,200.00	0.00	No	No
12	30/05/2015	Sally Brummitt	30/04/2015	Journal Opening Balance	O/Bals as at 01/05/15	Purchases - Boxed Games (5002)	2,465.00	0.00	No	No
12	30/05/2015	Sally Brummitt	30/04/2015	Journal Opening Balance	O/Bals as at 01/05/15	Office Stationery (7500)	53.00	0.00	No	No
12	30/05/2015	Sally Brummitt	30/04/2015	Journal Opening Balance	O/Bals as at 01/05/15	Electricity (7200)	167.00	0.00	No	No
12	30/05/2015	Sally Brummitt	30/04/2015	Journal Opening Balance	O/Bals as at 01/05/15	Rent and Rates (7100)	1,550.00	0.00	No	No
12	30/05/2015	Sally Brummitt	30/04/2015	Journal Opening Balance	O/Bals as at 01/05/15	Opening Balances Control Account (9998)	0.00	3,000.00	No	No

12	30/05/2015	Sally Brummitt	30/04/2015		Journal Opening Balance	O/Bals as at 01/05/15	Opening Balances Control Account (9998)	0.00	5,800.00	No	No
12	30/05/2015	Sally Brummitt	30/04/2015		Journal Opening Balance	O/Bals as at 01/05/15	VAT on Sales (2200)	0.00	543.00	No	No
12	30/05/2015	Sally Brummitt	30/04/2015		Journal Opening Balance	O/Bals as at 01/05/15	Opening Balances Control Account (9998)	0.00	109.00	No	No
12	30/05/2015	Sally Brummitt	30/04/2015		Journal Opening Balance	O/Bals as at 01/05/15	Capital (3000)	0.00	20,000.00	No	No
12	30/05/2015	Sally Brummitt	30/04/2015		Journal Opening Balance	O/Bals as at 01/05/15	Opening Balances Control Account (9998)	0.00	355.00	No	No
12	30/05/2015	Sally Brummitt	30/04/2015		Journal Opening Balance	O/Bals as at 01/05/15	Sales - Computer Games (4000)	0.00	6,080.00	No	No
12	30/05/2015	Sally Brummitt	30/04/2015		Journal Opening Balance	O/Bals as at 01/05/15	Sales - Jigsaws (4001)	0.00	700.00	No	No
12	30/05/2015	Sally Brummitt	30/04/2015		Journal Opening Balance	O/Bals as at 01/05/15	Sales - Boxed Games (4002)	0.00	1,967.00	No	No
12	30/05/2015	Sally Brummitt	30/04/2015		Journal Opening Balance	O/Bals as at 01/05/15	Opening Balances Control Account (9998)	0.00	8,000.00	No	No
12	30/05/2015	Sally Brummitt	30/04/2015		Journal Opening Balance	O/Bals as at 01/05/15	Opening Balances Control Account (9998)	0.00	3,200.00	No	No
12	30/05/2015	Sally Brummitt	30/04/2015		Journal Opening Balance	O/Bals as at 01/05/15	Opening Balances Control Account (9998)	0.00	2,465.00	No	No

12	30/05/2015	Sally Brummitt	30/04/2015	.	Journal Opening Balance	O/Bals as at 01/05/15	Opening Balances Control Account (9998)	0.00	53.00	No	No
12	30/05/2015	Sally Brummitt	30/04/2015		Journal Opening Balance	O/Bals as at 01/05/15	Opening Balances Control Account (9998)	0.00	167.00	No	No
12	30/05/2015	Sally Brummitt	30/04/2015		Journal Opening Balance	O/Bals as at 01/05/15	Opening Balances Control Account (9998)	0.00	1,550.00	No	No
13	30/05/2015	Sally Brummitt	01/05/2015		Bank Transfer	TRANS01	Current (1200)	0.00	500.00	Yes	No
13	30/05/2015	Sally Brummitt	01/05/2015		Bank Transfer	TRANS01	Deposit (1220)	500.00	0.00	No	No
14	30/05/2015	Sally Brummitt	04/05/2015	Busy Bee Toys (BB01)	Sales QE Invoice	2021	Sales - Computer Games (4000)	0.00	2,585.00	No	No
14	30/05/2015	Sally Brummitt	04/05/2015	Busy Bee Toys (BB01)	Sales QE Invoice	2021	VAT on Sales (2200)	0.00	517.00	No	No
14	30/05/2015	Sally Brummitt	04/05/2015	Busy Bee Toys (BB01)	Sales QE Invoice	2021	Trade Debtors (1100)	3,102.00	0.00	No	No
15	30/05/2015	Sally Brummitt	04/05/2015	Forming Fun (FF02)	Sales QE Invoice	2022	Sales - Boxed Games (4002)	0.00	500.00	No	No
15	30/05/2015	Sally Brummitt	04/05/2015	Forming Fun (FF02)	Sales QE Invoice	2022	VAT on Sales (2200)	0.00	100.00	No	No
15	30/05/2015	Sally Brummitt	04/05/2015	Forming Fun (FF02)	Sales QE Invoice	2022	Trade Debtors (1100)	600.00	0.00	No	No
16	30/05/2015	Sally Brummitt	06/05/2015	Teddy T's Party (TP04)	Sales QE Invoice	2023	Sales - Computer Games (4000)	0.00	5,000.00	No	No
16	30/05/2015	Sally Brummitt	06/05/2015	Teddy T's Party (TP04)	Sales QE Invoice	2023	VAT on Sales (2200)	0.00	1,000.00	No	No
16	30/05/2015	Sally Brummitt	06/05/2015	Teddy T's Party (TP04)	Sales QE Invoice	2023	Trade Debtors (1100)	6,000.00	0.00	No	No

17	30/05/2015	Sally Brummitt	13/05/2015	Teddy T's Party (TP04)	Sales QE Credit		CN101	Trade Debtors (1100)	0.00	384.00	No	No
17	30/05/2015	Sally Brummitt	13/05/2015	Teddy T's Party (TP04)	Sales QE Credit		CN101	Sales - Computer Games (4000)	320.00	0.00	No	No
17	30/05/2015	Sally Brummitt	13/05/2015	Teddy T's Party (TP04)	Sales QE Credit		CN101	VAT on Sales (2200)	64.00	0.00	No	No
18	30/05/2015	Sally Brummitt	03/05/2015	Abacus C & C (PL01)	Purchase QE Invoice		B/989	Purchases - Computer Games (5000)	450.00	0.00	No	No
18	30/05/2015	Sally Brummitt	03/05/2015	Abacus C & C (PL01)	Purchase QE Invoice		B/989	VAT on Purchases (2201)	90.00	0.00	No	No
18	30/05/2015	Sally Brummitt	03/05/2015	Abacus C & C (PL01)	Purchase QE Invoice		B/989	Trade Creditors (2100)	0.00	540.00	No	No
19	30/05/2015	Sally Brummitt	05/05/2015	Compugames Ltd (PL02)	Purchase QE Invoice		145215	Purchases - Boxed Games (5002)	500.00	0.00	No	No
19	30/05/2015	Sally Brummitt	05/05/2015	Compugames Ltd (PL02)	Purchase QE Invoice		145215	VAT on Purchases (2201)	100.00	0.00	No	No
19	30/05/2015	Sally Brummitt	05/05/2015	Compugames Ltd (PL02)	Purchase QE Invoice		145215	Trade Creditors (2100)	0.00	600.00	No	No
20	30/05/2015	Sally Brummitt	10/05/2015	Space Models (PL03)	Purchase QE Invoice		C-32632	Purchases - Computer Games (5000)	1,000.00	0.00	No	No
20	30/05/2015	Sally Brummitt	10/05/2015	Space Models (PL03)	Purchase QE Invoice		C-32632	VAT on Purchases (2201)	200.00	0.00	No	No
20	30/05/2015	Sally Brummitt	10/05/2015	Space Models (PL03)	Purchase QE Invoice		C-32632	Trade Creditors (2100)	0.00	1,200.00	No	No
21	30/05/2015	Sally Brummitt	10/05/2015	Toys Unlimited (PL04)	Purchase QE Invoice		12421	Purchases - Jigsaws (5001)	18.00	0.00	No	No
21	30/05/2015	Sally Brummitt	10/05/2015	Toys Unlimited (PL04)	Purchase QE Invoice		12421	Trade Creditors (2100)	0.00	18.00	No	No

22	30/05/2015	Sally Brummitt	15/05/2015	Compugames Ltd (PL02)	Purchase QE Credit		11245	Trade Creditors (2100)	105.60	0.00	No	No
22	30/05/2015	Sally Brummitt	15/05/2015	Compugames Ltd (PL02)	Purchase QE Credit		11245	Purchases - Computer Games (5000)	0.00	88.00	No	No
22	30/05/2015	Sally Brummitt	15/05/2015	Compugames Ltd (PL02)	Purchase QE Credit		11245	VAT on Purchases (2201)	0.00	17.60	No	No
23	30/05/2015	Sally Brummitt	17/05/2015	Busy Bee Toys (BB01)	Customer Receipt		Chq No. 100322	Current (1200)	349.20	0.00	Yes	No
23	30/05/2015	Sally Brummitt	17/05/2015	Busy Bee Toys (BB01)	Customer Receipt		Chq No. 100322	Trade Debtors (1100)	0.00	349.20	No	No
24	30/05/2015	Sally Brummitt	17/05/2015	Forming Fun (FF02)	Customer Receipt		Chq No. 267543	Current (1200)	99.60	0.00	No	Yes
24	30/05/2015	Sally Brummitt	17/05/2015	Forming Fun (FF02)	Customer Receipt		Chq No. 267543	Trade Debtors (1100)	0.00	99.60	No	Yes
24	30/05/2015	Sally Brummitt	17/05/2015	Forming Fun (FF02)	Customer Receipt		Chq No. 267543	Current (1200)	0.00	99.60	No	Yes
24	30/05/2015	Sally Brummitt	17/05/2015	Forming Fun (FF02)	Customer Receipt		Chq No. 267543	Trade Debtors (1100)	99.60	0.00	No	Yes
25	30/05/2015	Sally Brummitt	26/05/2015	Teddy T's Party (TP04)	Customer Receipt		BACS	Trade Debtors (1100)	384.00	0.00	No	No
25	30/05/2015	Sally Brummitt	26/05/2015	Teddy T's Party (TP04)	Customer Receipt		BACS	Current (1200)	195.60	0.00	Yes	No
25	30/05/2015	Sally Brummitt	26/05/2015	Teddy T's Party (TP04)	Customer Receipt		BACS	Trade Debtors (1100)	0.00	579.60	No	No
26	30/05/2015	Sally Brummitt	22/05/2015	Abacus C & C (PL01)	Supplier Payment		Chq No. 101333	Trade Creditors (2100)	369.60	0.00	No	Yes
26	30/05/2015	Sally Brummitt	22/05/2015	Abacus C & C (PL01)	Supplier Payment		Chq No. 101333	Current (1200)	0.00	369.60	No	Yes
26	30/05/2015	Sally Brummitt	22/05/2015	Abacus C & C (PL01)	Supplier Payment		Chq No. 101333	Trade Creditors (2100)	0.00	369.60	No	Yes
26	30/05/2015	Sally Brummitt	22/05/2015	Abacus C & C (PL01)	Supplier Payment		Chq No. 101333	Current (1200)	369.60	0.00	No	Yes
27	30/05/2015	Sally Brummitt	22/05/2015	Abacus C & C (PL01)	Supplier Payment		Chq No. 101333	Trade Creditors (2100)	369.60	0.00	No	No

27	30/05/2015	Sally Brummitt	22/05/2015	Abacus C & C (PL01)	Supplier Payment		Chq No. 101333	Current (1200)	0.00	369.60	Yes	No
28	30/05/2015	Sally Brummitt	22/05/2015	Compugames Ltd (PL02)	Supplier Payment		Chq No. 101334	Trade Creditors (2100)	511.20	0.00	No	No
28	30/05/2015	Sally Brummitt	22/05/2015	Compugames Ltd (PL02)	Supplier Payment		Chq No. 101334	Trade Creditors (2100)	600.00	0.00	No	No
28	30/05/2015	Sally Brummitt	22/05/2015	Compugames Ltd (PL02)	Supplier Payment		Chq No. 101334	Trade Creditors (2100)	0.00	105.60	No	No
28	30/05/2015	Sally Brummitt	22/05/2015	Compugames Ltd (PL02)	Supplier Payment		Chq No. 101334	Current (1200)	0.00	1,005.60	Yes	No
29	30/05/2015	Sally Brummitt	13/05/2015		Other Receipt		Cash Sale	Sales - Computer Games (4000)	0.00	1,000.00	No	No
29	30/05/2015	Sally Brummitt	13/05/2015		Other Receipt		Cash Sale	VAT on Sales (2200)	0.00	200.00	No	No
29	30/05/2015	Sally Brummitt	13/05/2015		Other Receipt		Cash Sale	Current (1200)	1,200.00	0.00	Yes	No
30	30/05/2015	Sally Brummitt	13/05/2015		Other Receipt		Cash Sale	Sales - Jigsaws (4001)	0.00	2,399.50	No	No
30	30/05/2015	Sally Brummitt	13/05/2015		Other Receipt		Cash Sale	VAT on Sales (2200)	0.00	479.90	No	No
30	30/05/2015	Sally Brummitt	13/05/2015		Other Receipt		Cash Sale	Current (1200)	2,879.40	0.00	Yes	No
31	30/05/2015	Sally Brummitt	20/05/2015		Other Receipt		Cash Sale	Sales - Computer Games (4000)	0.00	829.17	No	Yes
31	30/05/2015	Sally Brummitt	20/05/2015		Other Receipt		Cash Sale	VAT on Sales (2200)	0.00	165.83	No	Yes
31	30/05/2015	Sally Brummitt	20/05/2015		Other Receipt		Cash Sale	Current (1200)	995.00	0.00	No	Yes
31	30/05/2015	Sally Brummitt	20/05/2015		Other Receipt		Cash Sale	Sales - Computer Games (4000)	829.17	0.00	No	Yes
31	30/05/2015	Sally Brummitt	20/05/2015		Other Receipt		Cash Sale	VAT on Sales (2200)	165.83	0.00	No	Yes
31	30/05/2015	Sally Brummitt	20/05/2015		Other Receipt		Cash Sale	Current (1200)	0.00	995.00	No	Yes

32	30/05/2015	Sally Brummitt	20/05/2015		Other Payment		Voucher No. 012	Petty Cash (1210)	0.00	32.00	No	No
32	30/05/2015	Sally Brummitt	20/05/2015		Other Payment		Voucher No. 012	Subscriptions (8201)	32.00	0.00	No	No
33	30/05/2015	Sally Brummitt	21/05/2015		Other Payment		Voucher No. 013	Petty Cash (1210)	0.00	12.48	No	No
33	30/05/2015	Sally Brummitt	21/05/2015		Other Payment		Voucher No. 013	Refreshments (8205)	10.40	0.00	No	No
33	30/05/2015	Sally Brummitt	21/05/2015		Other Payment		Voucher No. 013	VAT on Purchases (2201)	2.08	0.00	No	No
34	30/05/2015	Sally Brummitt	25/05/2015		Journal		JNL02	Drawings (3260)	2,000.00	0.00	No	No
34	30/05/2015	Sally Brummitt	25/05/2015		Journal		JNL02	Current (1200)	0.00	2,000.00	Yes	No
35	30/05/2015	Sally Brummitt	20/05/2015		Other Receipt		Cash Sale	Sales - Computer Games (4000)	0.00	995.00	No	No
35	30/05/2015	Sally Brummitt	20/05/2015		Other Receipt		Cash Sale	Current (1200)	995.00	0.00	Yes	No
36	30/05/2015	Sally Brummitt	31/05/2015		Journal		JNL03	Electricity (7200)	502.00	0.00	No	No
36	30/05/2015	Sally Brummitt	31/05/2015		Journal		JNL03	Rent and Rates (7100)	0.00	502.00	No	No
37	30/05/2015	Sally Brummitt	28/05/2015	Space Models (PL03)	Supplier Payment		Chq No. 101335	Trade Creditors (2100)	306.00	0.00	No	No
37	30/05/2015	Sally Brummitt	28/05/2015	Space Models (PL03)	Supplier Payment		Chq No. 101335	Current (1200)	0.00	306.00	No	No
38	30/05/2015	Sally Brummitt	28/05/2015	Toys Unlimited (PL04)	Supplier Payment		Chq No. 101336	Trade Creditors (2100)	450.00	0.00	No	No
38	30/05/2015	Sally Brummitt	28/05/2015	Toys Unlimited (PL04)	Supplier Payment		Chq No. 101336	Current (1200)	0.00	450.00	Yes	No
39	30/05/2015	Sally Brummitt	28/05/2015	Abacus C & C (PL01)	Supplier Payment		BACS	Trade Creditors (2100)	540.00	0.00	No	No
39	30/05/2015	Sally Brummitt	28/05/2015	Abacus C & C (PL01)	Supplier Payment		BACS	Current (1200)	0.00	540.00	Yes	No
40	30/05/2015	Sally Brummitt	29/05/2015	Busy Bee Toys (BB01)	Customer Receipt		Chq No. 104662	Current (1200)	3,102.00	0.00	Yes	No

No	Posted	User	Date	Name	Type	Reference	Account	Debit	Credit		
40	30/05/2015	Sally Brummitt	29/05/2015	Busy Bee Toys (BB01)	Customer Receipt	Chq No. 104662	Trade Debtors (1100)	0.00	3,102.00	No	No
41	30/05/2015	Sally Brummitt	29/05/2015	Forming Fun (FF02)	Customer Receipt	Chq No. 828100	Current (1200)	400.00	0.00	Yes	No
41	30/05/2015	Sally Brummitt	29/05/2015	Forming Fun (FF02)	Customer Receipt	Chq No. 828100	Trade Debtors (1100)	0.00	400.00	No	No
42	30/05/2015	Sally Brummitt	29/05/2015	Teddy T's Party (TP04)	Customer Receipt	Chq No. 672522	Current (1200)	6,000.00	0.00	Yes	No
42	30/05/2015	Sally Brummitt	29/05/2015	Teddy T's Party (TP04)	Customer Receipt	Chq No. 672522	Trade Debtors (1100)	0.00	6,000.00	No	No
43	30/05/2015	Sally Brummitt	14/05/2015		Other Receipt	CSH41	Sales - Computer Games (4000)	0.00	220.00	No	No
43	30/05/2015	Sally Brummitt	14/05/2015		Other Receipt	CSH41	VAT on Sales (2200)	0.00	44.00	No	No
43	30/05/2015	Sally Brummitt	14/05/2015		Other Receipt	CSH41	Current (1200)	264.00	0.00	Yes	No
44	30/05/2015	Sally Brummitt	19/05/2015		Other Receipt	Debit Card	Other income (4900)	0.00	45.00	No	No
44	30/05/2015	Sally Brummitt	19/05/2015		Other Receipt	Debit Card	VAT on Sales (2200)	0.00	0.00	No	No
44	30/05/2015	Sally Brummitt	19/05/2015		Other Receipt	Debit Card	Current (1200)	45.00	0.00	Yes	No
45	30/05/2015	Sally Brummitt	17/05/2015	Forming Fun (FF02)	Customer Receipt	Chq No. 267543	Current (1200)	99.60	0.00	Yes	No
45	30/05/2015	Sally Brummitt	17/05/2015	Forming Fun (FF02)	Customer Receipt	Chq No. 267543	Trade Debtors (1100)	0.00	99.60	No	No
46	30/05/2015	Sally Brummitt	17/05/2015	Forming Fun (FF02)	Customer Refund	Bounced Cheque	Trade Debtors (1100)	99.60	0.00	No	No
46	30/05/2015	Sally Brummitt	17/05/2015	Forming Fun (FF02)	Customer Refund	Bounced Cheque	Current (1200)	0.00	99.60	Yes	No
47	30/05/2015	Sally Brummitt	05/05/2015		Other Payment	Direct Debit	Current (1200)	0.00	100.00	No	Yes
47	30/05/2015	Sally Brummitt	05/05/2015		Other Payment	Direct Debit	Insurance (7610)	100.00	0.00	No	Yes
47	30/05/2015	Sally Brummitt	05/05/2015		Other Payment	Direct Debit	VAT on Purchases (2201)	0.00	0.00	No	Yes

No	Posted	User	Date	Name	Type	Reference	Account	Debit	Credit		
47	30/05/2015	Sally Brummitt	05/05/2015		Other Payment	Direct Debit	Current (1200)	100.00	0.00	No	Yes
47	30/05/2015	Sally Brummitt	05/05/2015		Other Payment	Direct Debit	Insurance (7610)	0.00	100.00	No	Yes
47	30/05/2015	Sally Brummitt	05/05/2015		Other Payment	Direct Debit	VAT on Purchases (2201)	0.00	0.00	No	Yes
48	30/05/2015	Sally Brummitt	05/05/2015		Other Payment	Direct Debit	Current (1200)	0.00	100.00	No	Yes
48	30/05/2015	Sally Brummitt	05/05/2015		Other Payment	Direct Debit	Insurance (7610)	100.00	0.00	No	Yes
48	30/05/2015	Sally Brummitt	05/05/2015		Other Payment	Direct Debit	VAT on Purchases (2201)	0.00	0.00	No	Yes
48	30/05/2015	Sally Brummitt	05/05/2015		Other Payment	Direct Debit	Current (1200)	100.00	0.00	No	Yes
48	30/05/2015	Sally Brummitt	05/05/2015		Other Payment	Direct Debit	Insurance (7610)	0.00	100.00	No	Yes
48	30/05/2015	Sally Brummitt	05/05/2015		Other Payment	Direct Debit	VAT on Purchases (2201)	0.00	0.00	No	Yes
49	30/05/2015	Sally Brummitt	31/05/2015		Other Payment	Direct Debit	Current (1200)	0.00	100.00	Yes	No
49	30/05/2015	Sally Brummitt	31/05/2015		Other Payment	Direct Debit	Insurance (7610)	100.00	0.00	No	No
49	30/05/2015	Sally Brummitt	31/05/2015		Other Payment	Direct Debit	VAT on Purchases (2201)	0.00	0.00	No	No
50	30/05/2015	Sally Brummitt	31/05/2015		Bank Transfer	CSH25	Current (1200)	0.00	44.48	Yes	No
50	30/05/2015	Sally Brummitt	31/05/2015		Bank Transfer	CSH25	Petty Cash (1210)	44.48	0.00	No	No
51	30/05/2015	Sally Brummitt	31/05/2015		Journal	JNL04	Current (1200)	10,000.00	0.00	Yes	No
51	30/05/2015	Sally Brummitt	31/05/2015		Journal	JNL04	Loan Account (2500)	0.00	10,000.00	No	No
52	30/05/2015	Sally Brummitt	31/05/2015		Bank Payment	Bank Charge	Current (1200)	0.00	101.32	Yes	No
52	30/05/2015	Sally Brummitt	31/05/2015		Bank Payment	Bank Charge	Bank charges and interest (7900)	101.32	0.00	No	No

TASK 23

Aged Debtors (summary)

Toy Shop

Aged Debtors Report

To Date: 31/05/2015

Customer	Credit limit	O/S Amt	< 30 days	< 60 days	< 90 days	< 120 days	Older
Forming Fun (FF02)	£4,000.00	£299.60	£200.00	£99.60	£0.00	£0.00	£0.00
Space Models (SM03)	£3,000.00	£1,195.20	£0.00	£1,195.20	£0.00	£0.00	£0.00
TOTAL		£1,494.80	£200.00	£1,294.80	£0.00	£0.00	£0.00

PRACTICE PAPER 2

CRAZY HAIR ANSWERS

TASK 3.2

Customer Address List

Crazy Hair

Customer Address List

Address Types: All

Customer Name	Address	Contact name	Phone	Mobile	Email	Fax
Alfred Images (104)	Masuki Offices PO Box 5684 Birmingham B23 4RD United Kingdom	Main Contact				
Figgaro (110)	Beta Studio 34 Knightsbridge Way Morden SE23 4KA United Kingdom	Main Contact				
Blades (118)	Alpha Studio 45 Key West London SE1 0JF United Kingdom	Main Contact				
Hair Studio (122)	Framlington Court Lee London SE4 7YH United Kingdom	Main Contact				
Ribbons & Curls (138)	PO Box 1120 Canning Town London TN2 2EB United Kingdom	Main Contact				

TASK 3.2

Supplier Address List

Crazy Hair

Supplier Address List

Address Types: All

Supplier Name	Address	Contact name	Phone	Mobile	Email	Fax
Avada Cash & Carry (1134)	32 Surrey Quay Isle of Dogs E12 3NW United Kingdom	Main Contact				
Straightside Supplies (1138)	Havering Place Holborn London WC1 2PP United Kingdom	Main Contact				
Hair Supplies (1165)	43 St Helens Way London SE7 3RF United Kingdom	Main Contact				
Wig Specialists (1185)	Retro Square 32 Wigmore Road London EC1V 3SG United Kingdom	Main Contact				

TASK 3.2

Trial Balance

Crazy Hair

Trial Balance Report

From Date: 30/04/2015   To Date: 31/05/2015

Nominal Code	Name	Debits	Credits
0040	Furniture and fittings - Cost	31,000.00	
0050	Motor Vehicles - Cost	24,000.00	
1100	Trade Debtors	8,907.60	
1200	Current	54,210.81	
1210	Cash in Hand	200.00	
2100	Trade Creditors		7,214.40
2200	VAT on Sales		5,550.00
2201	VAT on Purchases	1,507.94	
3000	Capital		165,000.00
3260	Drawings	5,000.00	
4000	Sales - Brushes		345.00
4001	Sales - Combs		187.00
4002	Sales - Colours		3,801.45
4003	Sales - Hairdryers		758.00
4004	Sales - Wigs		5,600.00
4005	Cash Sales		617.50
5000	Purchases - Brushes	873.00	
5001	Purchases - Combs	50.00	
5002	Purchases - Colour	4,200.00	
5003	Purchases - Hairdryers	6,310.00	
5004	Purchases - Wigs	52,814.00	
	TOTAL	£189,073.35	£189,073.35

TASK 12

Trial Balance

Crazy Hair

Trial Balance Report

From Date: 30/04/2015   To Date: 31/05/2015

Nominal Code	Name	Debits	Credits
0040	Furniture and fittings - Cost	31,000.00	
0050	Motor Vehicles - Cost	24,000.00	
1100	Trade Debtors	5,964.33	
1200	Current	57,373.41	
1210	Petty Cash	155.17	
2100	Trade Creditors		7,341.96
2200	VAT on Sales		6,482.35
2201	VAT on Purchases	2,401.96	
3000	Capital		165,000.00
3260	Drawings	5,000.00	
4000	Sales - Brushes		1,204.30
4001	Sales - Combs		187.00
4002	Sales - Colours		4,172.85
4003	Sales - Hairdryers		1,621.40
4004	Sales - Wigs		8,167.68
4005	Cash Sales		617.50
5000	Purchases - Brushes	1,064.60	
5001	Purchases - Combs	50.00	
5002	Purchases - Colour	5,154.00	
5003	Purchases - Hairdyers	6,488.56	
5004	Purchases - Wigs	56,104.90	
7400	Travel and Entertainment	33.60	
7500	Office costs	4.51	
	TOTAL	£194,795.04	£194,795.04

TASK 12

Sales Day Book

Crazy Hair

Sales Day Book Report

From Date: 30/04/2015

To Date: 31/05/2015

Type: Sales QE Invoice

Trans ID	Type	Date	Name	Invoice Number	Ref	Details	Net	VAT	Total
14	Sales QE Invoice	12/05/2015	Ribbons & Curls		3353		141.00	28.20	169.20
15	Sales QE Invoice	12/05/2015	Alfred Images		3354		581.00	116.20	697.20
16	Sales QE Invoice	13/05/2015	Figgaro		3355		660.00	132.00	792.00
17	Sales QE Invoice	15/05/2015	Blades		3356		1,685.76	337.15	2,022.91
18	Sales QE Invoice	15/05/2015	Blades		3356		203.40	40.68	244.08
19	Sales QE Invoice	18/05/2015	Hair Studio		3357		316.80	63.36	380.16
20	Sales QE Invoice	18/05/2015	Hair Studio		3357		881.92	176.38	1,058.30
21	Sales QE Invoice	18/05/2015	Hair Studio		3357		230.40	46.08	276.48
						TOTAL	£4,700.28	£940.05	£5,640.33

TASK 12

Sales Returns Day Book

Crazy Hair

Sales Day Book Report

From Date: 30/04/2015

To Date: 31/05/2015

Type: Sales QE Credit

Trans ID	Type	Date	Name	Invoice Number	Ref	Details	Net	VAT	Total
22	Sales QE Credit	25/05/2015	Alfred Images		CN23		-56.00	-11.20	-67.20
						TOTAL	-£56.00	-£11.20	-£67.20

TASK 12

Purchase Day Book

Crazy Hair
Purchase Day Book Report

From Date: 30/04/2015

To Date: 31/05/2015

Type: Purchase QE Invoice

Trans ID	Type	Date	Name	Invoice Number	Ref	Details	Net	VAT	Total
23	Purchase QE Invoice	11/05/2015	Straightside Supplies		3362		191.60	38.32	229.92
24	Purchase QE Invoice	11/05/2015	Avada Cash & Carry		C/910		954.00	190.80	1,144.80
25	Purchase QE Invoice	13/05/2015	Hair Supplies		0814		178.56	0.00	178.56
26	Purchase QE Invoice	14/05/2015	Wig Specialists		S1198		3,393.60	678.72	4,072.32
						TOTAL	£4,717.76	£907.84	£5,625.60

TASK 12

Customer Activity Report

Crazy Hair
Customer Activity Report

From Date: 30/04/2015

To Date: 31/05/2015

Alfred Images (104)

Date	Number	Reference	Type	Net	VAT	Total	Discount	Outstanding
30/04/2015		Inv 3352	Customer OB Invoice	1,809.60	0.00	1,809.60		0.00
12/05/2015		3354	Sales QE Invoice	581.00	116.20	697.20		697.20
20/05/2015		Chq No. 183001	Customer Receipt			-1,809.60	0.00	0.00
25/05/2015		CN23	Sales QE Credit	-56.00	-11.20	-67.20		-67.20
						630.00		630.00

Figgaro (110)

Date	Number	Reference	Type	Net	VAT	Total	Discount	Outstanding
30/04/2015		Inv 2856	Customer OB Invoice	3,880.80	0.00	3,880.80		0.00
13/05/2015		3355	Sales QE Invoice	660.00	132.00	792.00		792.00
21/05/2015		BACS	Customer Receipt			-3,880.80	0.00	0.00

Sun 31 May 2015, 11:49

TASK 12

Customer Activity Report (continued)

						792.00		792.00

Blades (118)

Date	Number	Reference	Type	Net	VAT	Total	Discount	Outstanding
30/04/2015		Inv 3345	Customer OB Invoice	2,144.40	0.00	2,144.40		0.00
15/05/2015		3356	Sales QE Invoice	1,685.76	337.15	2,022.91		2,022.91
15/05/2015		3356	Sales QE Invoice	203.40	40.68	244.08		244.08
21/05/2015		Chq No. 654255	Customer Receipt			-2,144.40	0.00	0.00
						2,266.99		2,266.99

Hair Studio (122)

Date	Number	Reference	Type	Net	VAT	Total	Discount	Outstanding
30/04/2015		Inv 3098	Customer OB Invoice	681.60	0.00	681.60		0.00
18/05/2015		3357	Sales QE Invoice	316.80	63.36	380.16		380.16
18/05/2015		3357	Sales QE Invoice	881.92	176.38	1,058.30		1,058.30
18/05/2015		3357	Sales QE Invoice	230.40	46.08	276.48		276.48
21/05/2015		Chq No. 542221	Customer Receipt			-681.60	0.00	0.00
						1,714.94		1,714.94

Ribbons & Curls (138)

Date	Number	Reference	Type	Net	VAT	Total	Discount	Outstanding
30/04/2015		Inv 3123	Customer OB Invoice	391.20	0.00	391.20		391.20
12/05/2015		3353	Sales QE Invoice	141.00	28.20	169.20		169.20
						560.40		560.40

TASK 12

Supplier Activity Report

Crazy Hair

Supplier Activity Report

From Date: 30/04/2015

To Date: 31/05/2015

Avada Cash & Carry (1134)

Date	Number	Reference	Type	Net	VAT	Total	Discount	Outstanding
30/04/2015		C/251	Supplier OB Invoice	4,454.40	0.00	4,454.40		0.00
11/05/2015		C/910	Purchase QE Invoice	954.00	190.80	1,144.80		1,144.80
31/05/2015		Chq No. 163456	Supplier Payment			-4,454.40	0.00	0.00
						1,144.80		1,144.80

Straightside Supplies (1138)

Date	Number	Reference	Type	Net	VAT	Total	Discount	Outstanding
30/04/2015		9140	Supplier OB Invoice	1,839.60	0.00	1,839.60		1,839.60
11/05/2015		3362	Purchase QE Invoice	191.60	38.32	229.92		229.92
						2,069.52		2,069.52

Sun 31 May 2015, 11:53

Hair Supplies (1165)

Date	Number	Reference	Type	Net	VAT	Total	Discount	Outstanding
30/04/2015		0028	Supplier OB Invoice	818.40	0.00	818.40		0.00
13/05/2015		0814	Purchase QE Invoice	178.56	0.00	178.56		178.56
31/05/2015		Chq No. 163457	Supplier Payment			-818.40	0.00	0.00
						178.56		178.56

Wig Specialists (1185)

Date	Number	Reference	Type	Net	VAT	Total	Discount	Outstanding
30/04/2015		S653	Supplier OB Invoice	102.00	0.00	102.00		0.00
14/05/2015		S1198	Purchase QE Invoice	3,393.60	678.72	4,072.32		4,072.32
18/05/2015		C3223	Purchase QE Credit	-102.70	-20.54	-123.24		-123.24
31/05/2015		Chq No. 163455	Supplier Payment			-102.00	0.00	0.00
						3,949.08		3,949.08

TASK 12

Aged Creditors Report (summary)

Crazy Hair

Aged Creditors Report

To Date: 31/05/2015

Supplier	Credit limit	O/S Amt	< 30 days	< 60 days	< 90 days	< 120 days	Older
Avada Cash & Carry (1134)	£5,500.00	£1,144.80	£1,144.80	£0.00	£0.00	£0.00	£0.00
Hair Supplies (1165)	£4,000.00	£178.56	£178.56	£0.00	£0.00	£0.00	£0.00
Straightside Supplies (1138)	£12,000.00	£2,069.52	£229.92	£1,839.60	£0.00	£0.00	£0.00
Wig Specialists (1185)	£5,000.00	£3,949.08	£3,949.08	£0.00	£0.00	£0.00	£0.00
TOTAL		£7,341.96	£5,502.36	£1,839.60	£0.00	£0.00	£0.00

TASK 12

Aged Debtors Report (summary)

Crazy Hair

Aged Debtors Report

To Date: 31/05/2015

Customer	Credit limit	O/S Amt	< 30 days	< 60 days	< 90 days	< 120 days	Older
Alfred Images (104)	£8,000.00	£630.00	£630.00	£0.00	£0.00	£0.00	£0.00
Blades (118)	£6,100.00	£2,266.99	£2,266.99	£0.00	£0.00	£0.00	£0.00
Figgaro (110)	£6,500.00	£792.00	£792.00	£0.00	£0.00	£0.00	£0.00
Hair Studio (122)	£5,000.00	£1,714.94	£1,714.94	£0.00	£0.00	£0.00	£0.00
Ribbons & Curls (138)	£5,000.00	£560.40	£169.20	£391.20	£0.00	£0.00	£0.00
TOTAL		£5,964.33	£5,573.13	£391.20	£0.00	£0.00	£0.00

TASK 18

Customer Address List

Crazy Hair

Customer Address List

Address Types: All

Customer Name	Address	Contact name	Phone	Mobile	Email	Fax
Alfred Images (104)	Masuki Offices PO Box 5684 Birmingham B23 4RD United Kingdom	Main Contact				
Figgaro (110)	Beta Studio 34 Knightsbridge Way Morden SE23 4KA United Kingdom	Main Contact				
Blades (118)	Alpha Studio 45 Key West London SE1 0JF United Kingdom	Main Contact				
Hair Studio (122)	Framlington Court Lee London SE4 7YH United Kingdom	Main Contact				
Ribbons & Curls (138)	PO Box 1120 Canning Town London TN2 2EB United Kingdom	Main Contact				

TASK 18

Customer Activity

Crazy Hair
Customer Activity Report

From Date: 30/04/2015

To Date: 31/05/2015

Alfred Images (104)

Date	Number	Reference	Type	Net	VAT	Total	Discount	Outstanding
30/04/2015		Inv 3352	Customer OB Invoice	1,809.60	0.00	1,809.60		0.00
12/05/2015		3354	Sales QE Invoice	581.00	116.20	697.20		697.20
20/05/2015		Chq No. 183001	Customer Receipt			-1,809.60	0.00	0.00
25/05/2015		CN23	Sales QE Credit	-56.00	-11.20	-67.20		-67.20
						630.00		630.00

Figgaro (110)

Date	Number	Reference	Type	Net	VAT	Total	Discount	Outstanding
30/04/2015		Inv 2956	Customer OB Invoice	3,880.80	0.00	3,880.80		0.00
13/05/2015		3355	Sales QE Invoice	660.00	132.00	792.00		792.00
21/05/2015		BACS	Customer Receipt			-3,880.80	0.00	0.00
						792.00		792.00

Blades (118)

Date	Number	Reference	Type	Net	VAT	Total	Discount	Outstanding
30/04/2015		Inv 3345	Customer OB Invoice	2,144.40	0.00	2,144.40		0.00
15/05/2015		3356	Sales QE Invoice	1,685.76	337.15	2,022.91		2,022.91
15/05/2015		3356	Sales QE Invoice	203.40	40.68	244.08		244.08
21/05/2015		Chq No. 654255	Customer Receipt			-2,144.40	0.00	0.00
						2,266.99		2,266.99

Hair Studio (122)

Date	Number	Reference	Type	Net	VAT	Total	Discount	Outstanding
30/04/2015		Inv 3098	Customer OB Invoice	681.60	0.00	681.60		681.60
18/05/2015		3357	Sales QE Invoice	316.80	63.36	380.16		380.16
18/05/2015		3357	Sales QE Invoice	881.92	176.38	1,058.30		1,058.30
18/05/2015		3357	Sales QE Invoice	230.40	46.08	276.48		276.48
21/05/2015		Chq No. 542221	Customer Receipt			-681.60		0.00
21/05/2015		Bounced Cheque	Customer Refund			681.60		0.00
						2,396.54		2,396.54

Ribbons & Curls (138)

Date	Number	Reference	Type	Net	VAT	Total	Discount	Outstanding
30/04/2015		Inv 3123	Customer OB Invoice	391.20	0.00	391.20		391.20
12/05/2015		3353	Sales QE Invoice	141.00	28.20	169.20		169.20
						560.40		560.40

TASK 18

Supplier Activity

Crazy Hair

Supplier Activity Report

From Date: 30/04/2015

To Date: 31/05/2015

Avada Cash & Carry (1134)

Date	Number	Reference	Type	Net	VAT	Total	Discount	Outstanding
30/04/2015		C/251	Supplier OB Invoice	4,454.40	0.00	4,454.40		0.00
11/05/2015		C/910	Purchase QE Invoice	954.00	190.80	1,144.80		1,144.80
31/05/2015		Chq No. 163456	Supplier Payment			-4,454.40	0.00	0.00
						1,144.80		1,144.80

Straightside Supplies (1138)

Date	Number	Reference	Type	Net	VAT	Total	Discount	Outstanding
30/04/2015		9140	Supplier OB Invoice	1,839.60	0.00	1,839.60		1,839.60
11/05/2015		3382	Purchase QE Invoice	191.60	38.32	229.92		229.92
						2,069.52		2,069.52

Hair Supplies (1165)

Date	Number	Reference	Type	Net	VAT	Total	Discount	Outstanding
30/04/2015		0028	Supplier OB Invoice	818.40	0.00	818.40		0.00
13/05/2015		0814	Purchase QE Invoice	178.56	0.00	178.56		178.56
31/05/2015		Chq No. 163457	Supplier Payment			-818.40	0.00	0.00
						178.56		178.56

Wig Specialists (1185)

Date	Number	Reference	Type	Net	VAT	Total	Discount	Outstanding
30/04/2015		S653	Supplier OB Invoice	102.00	0.00	102.00		0.00
14/05/2015		S1198	Purchase QE Invoice	3,393.60	678.72	4,072.32		4,072.32
18/05/2015		C3223	Purchase QE Credit	-102.70	-20.54	-123.24		-123.24
31/05/2015		Chq No. 163455	Supplier Payment			-102.00	0.00	0.00
						3,949.08		3,949.08

TASK 18

Trial Balance for the month of May

Crazy Hair

Trial Balance Report

From Date: 30/04/2015   To Date: 31/05/2015

Nominal Code	Name	Debits	Credits
0040	Furniture and fittings - Cost	31,000.00	
0050	Motor Vehicles - Cost	24,000.00	
1100	Trade Debtors	6,645.93	
1200	Current	55,959.24	
1210	Petty Cash	185.69	
2100	Trade Creditors		7,341.96
2200	VAT on Sales		6,482.35
2201	VAT on Purchases	2,401.96	
3000	Capital		165,000.00
3260	Drawings	5,440.00	
4000	Sales - Brushes		1,204.30
4001	Sales - Combs		187.00
4002	Sales - Colours		4,172.85
4003	Sales - Hairdryers		1,621.40
4004	Sales - Wigs		8,167.68
4005	Cash Sales		617.50
5000	Purchases - Brushes	1,064.60	
5001	Purchases - Combs	50.00	
5002	Purchases - Colour	5,154.00	
5003	Purchases - Hairdyers	6,488.56	
5004	Purchases - Wigs	56,104.90	
7200	Electricity	66.94	
7400	Travel and Entertainment	33.60	
7500	Office costs	4.51	
7610	Premises Insurance	168.00	
7900	Bank charges and interest	27.11	
	TOTAL	£194,795.04	£194,795.04

TASK 18

Audit Trail for May only (summary & include opening balance)

Crazy Hair

Audit Trail Summary

From Date: 30/04/2015

To Date: 31/05/2015

Type: All

Transaction number	Entry Date	Created By	Trans Date	Name	Type	Invoice Number	Ref	Net	VAT	Total	Bank Reconciled
1	30/05/2015	Sally Brummitt	30/04/2015	Alfred Images (104)	Customer OB Invoice		Inv 3352	1,809.60	0.00	1,809.60	No
2	30/05/2015	Sally Brummitt	30/04/2015	Figgaro (110)	Customer OB Invoice		Inv 2856	3,880.80	0.00	3,880.80	No
3	30/05/2015	Sally Brummitt	30/04/2015	Blades (118)	Customer OB Invoice		Inv 3345	2,144.40	0.00	2,144.40	No
4	30/05/2015	Sally Brummitt	30/04/2015	Hair Studio (122)	Customer OB Invoice		Inv 3098	681.60	0.00	681.60	No
5	30/05/2015	Sally Brummitt	30/04/2015	Ribbons & Curls (138)	Customer OB Invoice		Inv 3123	391.20	0.00	391.20	No
6	31/05/2015	Sally Brummitt	30/04/2015	Avada Cash & Carry (1134)	Supplier OB Invoice		C/251	4,454.40	0.00	4,454.40	No
7	31/05/2015	Sally Brummitt	30/04/2015	Straightside Supplies (1138)	Supplier OB Invoice		9140	1,839.60	0.00	1,839.60	No
8	31/05/2015	Sally Brummitt	30/04/2015	Hair Supplies (1165)	Supplier OB Invoice		0028	818.40	0.00	818.40	No

9	31/05/2015	Sally Brummitt	30/04/2015	Wig Specialists (1185)	Supplier OB Invoice		S853	102.00	0.00	102.00	No
10	31/05/2015	Sally Brummitt	30/04/2015		Journal Opening Balance		O/Bal as at 01/05/15			55,000.00	No
11	31/05/2015	Sally Brummitt	30/04/2015		Bank Opening Balance					54,210.81	Yes
12	31/05/2015	Sally Brummitt	30/04/2015		Bank Opening Balance					200.00	No
13	31/05/2015	Sally Brummitt	30/04/2015		Journal Opening Balance		O/Bal as at 01/05/15			307,613.89	No
14	31/05/2015	Sally Brummitt	12/05/2015	Ribbons & Curls (138)	Sales QE Invoice		3353	141.00	28.20	169.20	No
15	31/05/2015	Sally Brummitt	12/05/2015	Alfred Images (104)	Sales QE Invoice		3354	581.00	116.20	697.20	No
16	31/05/2015	Sally Brummitt	13/05/2015	Figgaro (110)	Sales QE Invoice		3355	660.00	132.00	792.00	No
17	31/05/2015	Sally Brummitt	15/05/2015	Blades (118)	Sales QE Invoice		3356	1,685.76	337.15	2,022.91	No
18	31/05/2015	Sally Brummitt	15/05/2015	Blades (118)	Sales QE Invoice		3356	203.40	40.68	244.08	No
19	31/05/2015	Sally Brummitt	18/05/2015	Hair Studio (122)	Sales QE Invoice		3357	316.80	63.36	380.16	No
20	31/05/2015	Sally Brummitt	18/05/2015	Hair Studio (122)	Sales QE Invoice		3357	881.92	176.38	1,058.30	No
21	31/05/2015	Sally Brummitt	18/05/2015	Hair Studio (122)	Sales QE Invoice		3357	230.40	46.08	276.48	No
22	31/05/2015	Sally Brummitt	25/05/2015	Alfred Images (104)	Sales QE Credit		CN23	56.00	11.20	67.20	No
23	31/05/2015	Sally Brummitt	11/05/2015	Straightside Supplies (1138)	Purchase QE Invoice		3362	191.60	38.32	229.92	No
24	31/05/2015	Sally Brummitt	11/05/2015	Avada Cash & Carry (1134)	Purchase QE Invoice		C/910	954.00	190.80	1,144.80	No
25	31/05/2015	Sally Brummitt	13/05/2015	Hair Supplies (1165)	Purchase QE Invoice		0814	178.56	0.00	178.56	No

26	31/05/2015	Sally Brummitt	14/05/2015	Wig Specialists (1185)	Purchase QE Invoice	S1198	3,393.60	678.72	4,072.32	No
27	31/05/2015	Sally Brummitt	18/05/2015	Wig Specialists (1185)	Purchase QE Credit	C3223	102.70	20.54	123.24	No
28	31/05/2015	Sally Brummitt	20/05/2015	Alfred Images (104)	Customer Receipt	Chq No. 183001	1,809.60	0.00	1,809.60	Yes
29	31/05/2015	Sally Brummitt	21/05/2015	Blades (118)	Customer Receipt	Chq No. 654255	2,144.40	0.00	2,144.40	Yes
30	31/05/2015	Sally Brummitt	21/05/2015	Figgaro (110)	Customer Receipt	BACS	3,880.80	0.00	3,880.80	Yes
31	31/05/2015	Sally Brummitt	21/05/2015	Hair Studio (122)	Customer Receipt	Chq No. 542221	681.60	0.00	681.60	No
32	31/05/2015	Sally Brummitt	31/05/2015	Wig Specialists (1185)	Supplier Payment	Chq No. 163455	102.00	0.00	102.00	No
33	31/05/2015	Sally Brummitt	31/05/2015	Avada Cash & Carry (1134)	Supplier Payment	Chq No. 163456	4,454.40	0.00	4,454.40	No
34	31/05/2015	Sally Brummitt	31/05/2015	Hair Supplies (1165)	Supplier Payment	Chq No. 163457	818.40	0.00	818.40	No
35	31/05/2015	Sally Brummitt	19/05/2015		Other Payment	CSH 86	33.60	6.72	40.32	No
36	31/05/2015	Sally Brummitt	20/05/2015		Other Payment	CSH 87	4.51	0.00	4.51	No
37	31/05/2015	Sally Brummitt	20/05/2015		Other Receipt	1001	17.50	3.50	21.00	Yes
38	31/05/2015	Sally Brummitt	24/05/2015		Journal	JH12			440.00	Yes
39	31/05/2015	Sally Brummitt	21/05/2015	Hair Studio (122)	Customer Receipt	Chq No. 542221	681.60	0.00	681.60	Yes
40	31/05/2015	Sally Brummitt	21/05/2015	Hair Studio (122)	Customer Refund	Bounced Cheque	681.60	0.00	681.60	Yes
41	31/05/2015	Sally Brummitt	31/05/2015		Bank Transfer	TRF01			30.52	Yes
42	31/05/2015	Sally Brummitt	31/05/2015		Bank Payment	Bank Charge			27.11	Yes
43	31/05/2015	Sally Brummitt	24/05/2015		Other Payment	Direct Debit	168.00	0.00	168.00	Yes

Sun 31 May 2015, 12:43

| 44 | 31/05/2015 | Sally Brummitt | 31/05/2015 | | Other Payment | Direct Debit | 66.94 | 0.00 | 66.94 | Yes |

TASK 18

Aged Creditors (summary)

Crazy Hair

Aged Creditors Report

To Date: 31/05/2015

Supplier	Credit limit	O/S Amt	< 30 days	< 60 days	< 90 days	< 120 days	Older
Avada Cash & Carry (1134)	£5,500.00	£1,144.80	£1,144.80	£0.00	£0.00	£0.00	£0.00
Hair Supplies (1165)	£4,000.00	£178.56	£178.56	£0.00	£0.00	£0.00	£0.00
Straightside Supplies (1138)	£12,000.00	£2,069.52	£229.92	£1,839.60	£0.00	£0.00	£0.00
Wig Specialists (1185)	£5,000.00	£3,949.08	£3,949.08	£0.00	£0.00	£0.00	£0.00
TOTAL		£7,341.96	£5,502.36	£1,839.60	£0.00	£0.00	£0.00

TASK 18

Aged Debtors (summary)

Crazy Hair

Aged Debtors Report

To Date: 31/05/2015

Customer	Credit limit	O/S Amt	< 30 days	< 60 days	< 90 days	< 120 days	Older
Alfred Images (104)	£8,000.00	£630.00	£630.00	£0.00	£0.00	£0.00	£0.00
Blades (118)	£6,100.00	£2,266.99	£2,266.99	£0.00	£0.00	£0.00	£0.00
Figgaro (110)	£6,500.00	£792.00	£792.00	£0.00	£0.00	£0.00	£0.00
Hair Studio (122)	£5,000.00	£2,396.54	£1,714.94	£681.60	£0.00	£0.00	£0.00
Ribbons & Curls (138)	£5,000.00	£560.40	£169.20	£391.20	£0.00	£0.00	£0.00
TOTAL		**£6,645.93**	**£5,573.13**	**£1,072.80**	**£0.00**	**£0.00**	**£0.00**

TASK 18

Nominal Ledger Activity Report for Bank Current Account and Petty Cash Account

Crazy Hair

Detailed Nominal Activity: Current (1200)
30 April, 2015 - 31 May, 2015

Transaction Type: All

Transaction number	Date	Invoice Number	Name	Type	Reference	Description	Debit	Credit
11	30/04/2015			Bank Opening Balance				54,210.81
37	20/05/2015			Other Receipt	1001			21.00
28	20/05/2015		Alfred Images (104)	Customer Receipt	Chq No. 183001			1,809.60
40	21/05/2015		Hair Studio (122)	Customer Refund	Bounced Cheque		681.60	
30	21/05/2015		Figgaro (110)	Customer Receipt	BACS			3,880.80
39	21/05/2015		Hair Studio (122)	Customer Receipt	Chq No. 542221			681.60
29	21/05/2015		Blades (118)	Customer Receipt	Chq No. 654255			2,144.40
38	24/05/2015			Journal	JH12		440.00	
43	24/05/2015			Other Payment	Direct Debit		168.00	
34	31/05/2015		Hair Supplies (1165)	Supplier Payment	Chq No. 163457		818.40	
41	31/05/2015			Bank Transfer	TRF01		30.52	
32	31/05/2015		Wig Specialists (1185)	Supplier Payment	Chq No. 163455		102.00	
42	31/05/2015			Bank Payment	Bank Charge		27.11	
44	31/05/2015			Other Payment	Direct Debit		66.94	
33	31/05/2015		Avada Cash & Carry (1134)	Supplier Payment	Chq No. 163456		4,454.40	

Crazy Hair

Detailed Nominal Activity: Petty Cash (1210)
30 April, 2015 - 31 May, 2015

Transaction Type: All

Transaction number	Date	Invoice Number	Name	Type	Reference	Description	Debit	Credit
12	30/04/2015			Bank Opening Balance			200.00	
35	19/05/2015			Other Payment	CSH 86			40.32
36	20/05/2015			Other Payment	CSH 87			4.51
41	31/05/2015			Bank Transfer	TRF01		30.52	

PRACTICE PAPER 3

SHOES 4U ANSWERS

TASK 3.3

Customer Address List

Shoes 4U

Customer Address List

Address Types: All

Customer Name	Address	Contact name	Phone	Mobile	Email	Fax
Beckers Gate Ltd (SL186)	Butchergate Carlisle Cumbria C41 1SG United Kingdom	Main Contact				
Eaton Bowls Club (SL213)	Seaton Street St Neots Cambs PE19 8EF United Kingdom	Main Contact				
Jones Footwear (SL302)	Scotby Village Carlisle Cumbria C44 8BP United Kingdom	Main Contact				
Dickens Ladies Footwear (SL307)	17 Royal Square Bleachfield North Yorkshire YO87 9AD United Kingdom	Main Contact				

TASK 3.3

Supplier Address List

Shoes 4U

Supplier Address List

Address Types: All

Supplier Name	Address	Contact name	Phone	Mobile	Email	Fax
Bootsy & Smudge Ltd (PL112)	Factory Road Stilton Cambs PE7 3RP United Kingdom	Main Contact				
Briggsthorpe Boots (PL168)	Long Buckby Wharf Long Buckby Northampton NN4 9UW United Kingdom	Main Contact				
Gallows Fashion (PL172)	18 The Crescent Pickford Cambs PE7 8QV United Kingdom	Main Contact				
Dickens Ladies Footwear (PL173)	17 Royal Square Bleachfield North Yorkshire YO87 9AD United Kingdom	Main Contact				

TASK 3.3

Trial Balance

Shoes 4U

Trial Balance Report

From Date: 31/05/2015   To Date: 30/06/2015

Nominal Code	Name	Debits	Credits
0030	Freehold Property - Cost	72,000.00	
0040	Furniture and Fixtures - Cost	9,000.00	
0050	Motor Vehicles - Cost	7,500.00	
1100	Trade Debtors	10,386.27	
1200	Current	14,363.00	
1210	Cash In Hand	200.00	
1220	Deposit	5,000.00	
2100	Trade Creditors		47,048.26
2200	VAT on Sales		3,402.35
2201	VAT on Purchases	1,130.00	
3000	Capital		30,000.00
3260	Drawings	600.00	
4000	Sales - Men's Footwear		79,320.00
4001	Sales - Ladies Footwear		43,210.00
4002	Cash Sales		6,798.00
5000	Purchases - Men's Footwear	55,432.00	
5001	Purchases - Ladies Footwear	23,410.00	
6200	Advertising	7,231.00	
7100	Rent and rates	1,263.00	
7200	Electricity	567.34	
7500	Telephone	866.00	
7501	Office Stationery	830.00	

	TOTAL	£209,778.61	£209,778.61

TASK 10

Trial Balance

Shoes 4U

Trial Balance Report

From Date: 31/05/2015   To Date: 30/06/2015

Nominal Code	Name	Debits	Credits
0030	Freehold Property - Cost	72,000.00	
0040	Furniture and Fixtures - Cost	9,000.00	
0050	Motor Vehicles - Cost	7,500.00	
1100	Trade Debtors	6,874.56	
1200	Current	319.80	
1210	Cash In Hand	200.00	
1220	Deposit	5,000.00	
2100	Trade Creditors		29,948.26
2200	VAT on Sales		4,430.43
2201	VAT on Purchases	2,232.25	
3000	Capital		30,000.00
3260	Drawings	600.00	
4000	Sales - Men's Footwear		81,669.66
4001	Sales - Ladies Footwear		46,000.75
4002	Cash Sales		6,798.00
5000	Purchases - Men's Footwear	60,432.00	
5001	Purchases - Ladies Footwear	23,910.00	
6200	Advertising	7,231.00	
7100	Rent and rates	1,263.00	
7200	Electricity	567.34	
7500	Telephone	866.00	
7501	Office Stationery	841.25	
7502	Refreshment	9.90	
	TOTAL	**£198,847.10**	**£198,847.10**

TASK 10

Sales Day Book

Shoes 4U

Sales Day Book Report

From Date: 31/05/2015

To Date: 30/06/2015

Type: Sales QE Invoice

Trans ID	Type	Date	Name	Invoice Number	Ref	Details	Net	VAT	Total
13	Sales QE Invoice	04/06/2015	Beckers Gate Ltd		1622		450.00	90.00	540.00
14	Sales QE Invoice	06/06/2015	Eaton Bowls Club		1623		1,385.00	277.00	1,662.00
15	Sales QE Invoice	14/06/2015	Dickens Ladies Footwear		1624		450.00	90.00	540.00
16	Sales QE Invoice	14/06/2015	Dickens Ladies Footwear		1624		1,850.00	370.00	2,220.00
17	Sales QE Invoice	17/06/2015	Jones Footwear		1625		1,175.75	235.15	1,410.90
						TOTAL	£5,310.75	£1,062.15	£6,372.90

TASK 10

Customer Activity Report

Shoes 4U

Customer Activity Report

From Date: 31/05/2015

To Date: 30/06/2015

Beckers Gate Ltd (SL186)

Date	Number	Reference	Type	Net	VAT	Total	Discount	Outstanding
31/05/2015		1613	Customer OB Invoice	4,811.88	0.00	4,811.88		0.00
04/06/2015		1622	Sales QE Invoice	450.00	90.00	540.00		540.00
11/06/2015		Chq No. 199846	Customer Receipt			-4,811.88	0.00	0.00
						540.00		540.00

Eaton Bowls Club (SL213)

Date	Number	Reference	Type	Net	VAT	Total	Discount	Outstanding
31/05/2015		1582	Customer OB Invoice	961.98	0.00	961.98		0.00
06/06/2015		1623	Sales QE Invoice	1,385.00	277.00	1,662.00		1,662.00
14/06/2015		Chq No. 107654	Customer Receipt			-961.98	0.00	0.00
						1,662.00		1,662.00

TASK 10

Customer Activity Report (cont.)

Jones Footwear (SL302)

Date	Number	Reference	Type	Net	VAT	Total	Discount	Outstanding
31/05/2015		1596	Customer OB Invoice	3,828.75	0.00	3,828.75		0.00
14/06/2015		Chq No.244536	Customer Receipt			-3,828.75	0.00	0.00
17/06/2015		1625	Sales QE Invoice	1,175.75	235.15	1,410.90		1,410.90
						1,410.90		**1,410.90**

Dickens Ladies Footwear (SL307)

Date	Number	Reference	Type	Net	VAT	Total	Discount	Outstanding
31/05/2015		1601	Customer OB Invoice	783.66	0.00	783.66		783.66
08/06/2015		CR10	Sales QE Credit	-235.00	-47.00	-282.00		-282.00
14/06/2015		1624	Sales QE Invoice	450.00	90.00	540.00		540.00
14/06/2015		1624	Sales QE Invoice	1,850.00	370.00	2,220.00		2,220.00
						3,261.66		**3,261.66**

TASK 10

Supplier Activity Report

Shoes 4U

Supplier Activity Report

From Date: 31/05/2015

To Date: 30/06/2015

Bootsy & Smudge Ltd (PL112)

Date	Number	Reference	Type	Net	VAT	Total	Discount	Outstanding
31/05/2015		B/468	Supplier OB Invoice	2,881.26	0.00	2,881.26		2,881.26
02/06/2015		B/752	Purchase QE Invoice	300.00	60.00	360.00		360.00
13/06/2015		B/753	Purchase QE Invoice	200.00	40.00	240.00		240.00
						3,481.26		**3,481.26**

Briggsthorpe Boots (PL168)

Date	Number	Reference	Type	Net	VAT	Total	Discount	Outstanding
31/05/2015		0001087	Supplier OB Invoice	43,200.00	0.00	43,200.00		19,900.00
10/06/2015		12350	Purchase QE Invoice	2,500.00	500.00	3,000.00		3,000.00
18/06/2015		Chq No. 109888	Supplier Payment			-23,300.00	0.00	0.00
						22,900.00		**22,900.00**

Gallows Fashion (PL172)

Date	Number	Reference	Type	Net	VAT	Total	Discount	Outstanding
31/05/2015		G-01239	Supplier OB Invoice	400.00	0.00	400.00		0.00
10/06/2015		G-2285	Purchase QE Invoice	2,500.00	500.00	3,000.00		3,000.00
18/06/2015		Chq No. 109887	Supplier Payment			-400.00	0.00	0.00
						3,000.00		3,000.00

Dickens Ladies Footwear (PL173)

Date	Number	Reference	Type	Net	VAT	Total	Discount	Outstanding
31/05/2015		06345	Supplier OB Invoice	567.00	0.00	567.00		567.00
						567.00		567.00

TASK 10

Aged Creditors Report (detailed)

Shoes 4U

Aged Creditors Breakdown

To Date: 30/06/2015

Supplier	Date	Reference	Total	O/S Amt	< 30 days	< 60 days	< 90 days	< 120 days	Older
Bootsy & Smudge Ltd (PL112) Credit limit: £4,000.00 Terms: 30 days									
	31/05/2015	B/468	2,881.26	2,881.26		2,881.26			
	02/06/2015	B/752	360.00	360.00	360.00				
	13/06/2015	B/753	240.00	240.00	240.00				
			£3,481.26	£600.00	£2,881.26	£0.00	£0.00	£0.00	
Briggsthorpe Boots (PL168) Credit limit: £50,000.00 Terms: 30 days									
	31/05/2015	0001087	43,200.00	19,900.00		19,900.00			
	10/06/2015	12350	3,000.00	3,000.00	3,000.00				
			£22,900.00	£3,000.00	£19,900.00	£0.00	£0.00	£0.00	
Dickens Ladies Footwear (PL173) Credit limit: £2,000.00 Terms: 30 days									
	31/05/2015	06345	567.00	567.00		567.00			
			£567.00	£0.00	£567.00	£0.00	£0.00	£0.00	

Mon 01 Jun 2015, 12:11   Page 1 of 2

Gallows Fashion (PL172) Credit limit: £2,000.00 Terms: 30 days									
	10/06/2015	G-2285	3,000.00	3,000.00	3,000.00				
			£3,000.00	£3,000.00	£0.00	£0.00	£0.00	£0.00	
		TOTAL	£29,948.26	£6,600.00	£23,348.26	£0.00	£0.00	£0.00	

TASK 10

Aged Debtors Report (detailed)

Shoes 4U

Aged Debtors Breakdown

To Date: 30/06/2015

Customer	Date	Reference	Total	O/S Amt	< 30 days	< 60 days	< 90 days	< 120 days	Older
Beckers Gate Ltd (SL186)									
Credit limit: £5,000.00									
Terms: 30 days									
	04/06/2015	QE-1622	540.00	540.00	540.00				
			£540.00	£540.00	£0.00	£0.00	£0.00	£0.00	
Dickens Ladies Footwear (SL307)									
Credit limit: £11,000.00									
Terms: 30 days									
	31/05/2015	OB-1601	783.66	783.66		783.66			
	14/06/2015	QE-1624	540.00	540.00	540.00				
	14/06/2015	QE-1624	2,220.00	2,220.00	2,220.00				
	08/06/2015	QE-CR10	-282.00	-282.00	-282.00				
			£3,261.66	£2,478.00	£783.66	£0.00	£0.00	£0.00	
Eaton Bowls Club (SL213)									
Credit limit: £3,000.00									
Terms: 30 days									
	06/06/2015	QE-1623	1,662.00	1,662.00	1,662.00				
			£1,662.00	£1,662.00	£0.00	£0.00	£0.00	£0.00	

Mon 01 Jun 2015, 12:13 Page 1 of 2

Customer	Date	Reference	Total	O/S Amt	< 30 days	< 60 days	< 90 days	< 120 days	Older
Jones Footwear (SL302)									
Credit limit: £6,000.00									
Terms: 30 days									
	17/06/2015	QE-1625	1,410.90	1,410.90	1,410.90				
			£1,410.90	£1,410.90	£0.00	£0.00	£0.00	£0.00	
		TOTAL	£6,874.56	£6,090.90	£783.66	£0.00	£0.00	£0.00	

TASK 10

Nominal Ledger Activity Report for Bank Current Account and Petty Cash Account

Shoes 4U

Detailed Nominal Activity: Current (1200)
31 May, 2015 - 30 June, 2015

Transaction Type: All

Transaction number	Date	Invoice Number	Name	Type	Reference	Description	Debit	Credit
9	31/05/2015			Bank Opening Balance			19,363.00	
11	01/06/2015			Bank Transfer	TRF01			5,000.00
30	10/06/2015			Bank Transfer	TRF02			23.40
23	11/06/2015		Beckers Gate Ltd (SL186)	Customer Receipt	Chq No. 199846		4,811.88	
25	14/06/2015		Jones Footwear (SL302)	Customer Receipt	Chq No.244536		3,828.75	
24	14/06/2015		Eaton Bowls Club (SL213)	Customer Receipt	Chq No. 107654		961.98	
26	18/06/2015		Gallows Fashion (PL172)	Supplier Payment	Chq No. 109887			400.00
27	18/06/2015		Briggsthorpe Boots (PL168)	Supplier Payment	Chq No. 109888			23,300.00
31	23/06/2015			Other Receipt	F027		77.59	

Shoes 4U

Detailed Nominal Activity: Cash in Hand (1210)
31 May, 2015 - 30 June, 2015

Transaction Type: All

Transaction number	Date	Invoice Number	Name	Type	Reference	Description	Debit	Credit
10	31/05/2015			Bank Opening Balance			200.00	
28	05/06/2015			Other Payment	PCV 010			9.90
30	10/06/2015			Bank Transfer	TRF02		23.40	
29	10/06/2015			Other Payment	PCV 011			13.50

TASK 17

Trial Balance

Shoes 4U

Trial Balance Report

From Date: 31/05/2015   To Date: 30/06/2015

Nominal Code	Name	Debits	Credits
0030	Freehold Property - Cost	72,000.00	
0040	Furniture and Fixtures - Cost	9,000.00	
0050	Motor Vehicles - Cost	7,500.00	
1100	Trade Debtors	5,212.56	
1200	Current		2,531.18
1210	Cash in Hand	200.00	
1220	Deposit	5,000.00	
2100	Trade Creditors		29,948.26
2200	VAT on Sales		4,439.43
2201	VAT on Purchases	2,232.25	
3000	Capital		30,000.00
3260	Drawings	3,800.00	
4000	Sales - Men's Footwear		81,669.66
4001	Sales - Ladies Footwear		46,045.75
4002	Cash Sales		6,798.00
4900	Rent Income		1,500.00
5000	Purchases - Men's Footwear	60,432.00	
5001	Purchases - Ladies Footwear	23,910.00	
6200	Advertising	7,231.00	
7100	Rent and rates	1,263.00	
7200	Electricity	760.34	
7500	Telephone	866.00	
7501	Office Stationery	841.25	
7502	Refreshment	9.90	
7900	Bank charges and interest	50.00	
8100	Bad Debts	2,623.98	
	TOTAL	£202,932.28	£202,932.28

TASK 17

Audit Trail

Shoes 4U

Audit Trail Breakdown

From Date: 31/05/2015

To Date: 30/06/2015

Type: All

Trans ID	Entry Date	Created By	Trans Date	Name	Type	Invoice Number	Ref	Ledger Account	Debit	Credit	Bank Reconciled	Deleted
1	31/05/2015	Sally Brummitt	31/05/2015	Beckers Gate Ltd (SL186)	Customer OB Invoice		1613	Opening Balances Control Account (9998)	0.00	4,811.88	No	No
1	31/05/2015	Sally Brummitt	31/05/2015	Beckers Gate Ltd (SL186)	Customer OB Invoice		1613	Trade Debtors (1100)	4,811.88	0.00	No	No
2	31/05/2015	Sally Brummitt	31/05/2015	Eaton Bowls Club (SL213)	Customer OB Invoice		1582	Opening Balances Control Account (9998)	0.00	961.98	No	No
2	31/05/2015	Sally Brummitt	31/05/2015	Eaton Bowls Club (SL213)	Customer OB Invoice		1582	Trade Debtors (1100)	961.98	0.00	No	No
3	31/05/2015	Sally Brummitt	31/05/2015	Jones Footwear (SL302)	Customer OB Invoice		1596	Opening Balances Control Account (9998)	0.00	3,828.75	No	No
3	31/05/2015	Sally Brummitt	31/05/2015	Jones Footwear (SL302)	Customer OB Invoice		1596	Trade Debtors (1100)	3,828.75	0.00	No	No

Trans ID	Entry Date	Created By	Trans Date	Name	Type	Invoice Number	Ref	Ledger Account	Debit	Credit	Bank Reconciled	Deleted
4	31/05/2015	Sally Brummitt	31/05/2015	Dickens Ladies Footwear (SL307)	Customer OB Invoice		1601	Opening Balances Control Account (9998)	0.00	783.66	No	No
4	31/05/2015	Sally Brummitt	31/05/2015	Dickens Ladies Footwear (SL307)	Customer OB Invoice		1601	Trade Debtors (1100)	783.66	0.00	No	No
5	31/05/2015	Sally Brummitt	31/05/2015	Bootsy & Smudge Ltd (PL112)	Supplier OB Invoice		B/468	Opening Balances Control Account (9998)	2,881.26	0.00	No	No
5	31/05/2015	Sally Brummitt	31/05/2015	Bootsy & Smudge Ltd (PL112)	Supplier OB Invoice		B/468	Trade Creditors (2100)	0.00	2,881.26	No	No
6	31/05/2015	Sally Brummitt	31/05/2015	Briggsthorpe Boots (PL168)	Supplier OB Invoice		0001087	Opening Balances Control Account (9998)	43,200.00	0.00	No	No
6	31/05/2015	Sally Brummitt	31/05/2015	Briggsthorpe Boots (PL168)	Supplier OB Invoice		0001087	Trade Creditors (2100)	0.00	43,200.00	No	No
7	31/05/2015	Sally Brummitt	31/05/2015	Gallows Fashion (PL172)	Supplier OB Invoice		G-01239	Opening Balances Control Account (9998)	400.00	0.00	No	No
7	31/05/2015	Sally Brummitt	31/05/2015	Gallows Fashion (PL172)	Supplier OB Invoice		G-01239	Trade Creditors (2100)	0.00	400.00	No	No
8	31/05/2015	Sally Brummitt	31/05/2015	Dickens Ladies Footwear (PL173)	Supplier OB Invoice		06345	Opening Balances Control Account (9998)	567.00	0.00	No	No
8	31/05/2015	Sally Brummitt	31/05/2015	Dickens Ladies Footwear (PL173)	Supplier OB Invoice		06345	Trade Creditors (2100)	0.00	567.00	No	No
9	01/06/2015	Sally Brummitt	31/05/2015		Bank Opening Balance			Opening Balances Control Account (9998)	0.00	19,363.00	No	No

---

9	01/06/2015	Sally Brummitt	31/05/2015		Bank Opening Balance		Current (1200)	19,363.00	0.00	Yes	No
10	01/06/2015	Sally Brummitt	31/05/2015		Bank Opening Balance		Opening Balances Control Account (9998)	0.00	200.00	No	No
10	01/06/2015	Sally Brummitt	31/05/2015		Bank Opening Balance		Cash in Hand (1210)	200.00	0.00	No	No
11	01/06/2015	Sally Brummitt	01/06/2015		Bank Transfer	TRF01	Current (1200)	0.00	5,000.00	Yes	No
11	01/06/2015	Sally Brummitt	01/06/2015		Bank Transfer	TRF01	Deposit (1220)	5,000.00	0.00	No	No
12	01/06/2015	Sally Brummitt	31/05/2015		Journal Opening Balance	O/Bal as at 01/06/15	Freehold Property - Cost (0030)	72,000.00	0.00	No	No
12	01/06/2015	Sally Brummitt	31/05/2015		Journal Opening Balance	O/Bal as at 01/06/15	Motor Vehicles - Cost (0050)	7,500.00	0.00	No	No
12	01/06/2015	Sally Brummitt	31/05/2015		Journal Opening Balance	O/Bal as at 01/06/15	Furniture and Fixtures - Cost (0040)	9,000.00	0.00	No	No
12	01/06/2015	Sally Brummitt	31/05/2015		Journal Opening Balance	O/Bal as at 01/06/15	Opening Balances Control Account (9998)	3,402.35	0.00	No	No
12	01/06/2015	Sally Brummitt	31/05/2015		Journal Opening Balance	O/Bal as at 01/06/15	VAT on Purchases (2201)	1,130.00	0.00	No	No
12	01/06/2015	Sally Brummitt	31/05/2015		Journal Opening Balance	O/Bal as at 01/06/15	Opening Balances Control Account (9998)	30,000.00	0.00	No	No
12	01/06/2015	Sally Brummitt	31/05/2015		Journal Opening Balance	O/Bal as at 01/06/15	Drawings (3260)	600.00	0.00	No	No
12	01/06/2015	Sally Brummitt	31/05/2015		Journal Opening Balance	O/Bal as at 01/06/15	Opening Balances Control Account (9998)	79,320.00	0.00	No	No

12	01/06/2015	Sally Brummitt	31/05/2015		Journal Opening Balance	O/Bal as at 01/06/15	Opening Balances Control Account (9998)	43,210.00	0.00	No	No
12	01/06/2015	Sally Brummitt	31/05/2015		Journal Opening Balance	O/Bal as at 01/06/15	Opening Balances Control Account (9998)	6,798.00	0.00	No	No
12	01/06/2015	Sally Brummitt	31/05/2015		Journal Opening Balance	O/Bal as at 01/06/15	Purchases - Men's Footwear (5000)	55,432.00	0.00	No	No
12	01/06/2015	Sally Brummitt	31/05/2015		Journal Opening Balance	O/Bal as at 01/06/15	Purchases - Ladies Footwear (5001)	23,410.00	0.00	No	No
12	01/06/2015	Sally Brummitt	31/05/2015		Journal Opening Balance	O/Bal as at 01/06/15	Advertising (6200)	7,231.00	0.00	Yes	No
12	01/06/2015	Sally Brummitt	31/05/2015		Journal Opening Balance	O/Bal as at 01/06/15	Telephone (7500)	866.00	0.00	No	No
12	01/06/2015	Sally Brummitt	31/05/2015		Journal Opening Balance	O/Bal as at 01/06/15	Rent and rates (7100)	1,263.00	0.00	No	No
12	01/06/2015	Sally Brummitt	31/05/2015		Journal Opening Balance	O/Bal as at 01/06/15	Electricity (7200)	567.34	0.00	No	No
12	01/06/2015	Sally Brummitt	31/05/2015		Journal Opening Balance	O/Bal as at 01/06/15	Office Stationery (7501)	830.00	0.00	No	No
12	01/06/2015	Sally Brummitt	31/05/2015		Journal Opening Balance	O/Bal as at 01/06/15	Opening Balances Control Account (9998)	0.00	72,000.00	No	No
12	01/06/2015	Sally Brummitt	31/05/2015		Journal Opening Balance	O/Bal as at 01/06/15	Opening Balances Control Account (9998)	0.00	7,500.00	No	No

12	01/06/2015	Sally Brummitt	31/05/2015		Journal Opening Balance		O/Bal as at 01/06/15	Opening Balances Control Account (9998)	0.00	9,000.00	No	No
12	01/06/2015	Sally Brummitt	31/05/2015		Journal Opening Balance		O/Bal as at 01/06/15	VAT on Sales (2200)	0.00	3,402.35	No	No
12	01/06/2015	Sally Brummitt	31/05/2015		Journal Opening Balance		O/Bal as at 01/06/15	Opening Balances Control Account (9998)	0.00	1,130.00	No	No
12	01/06/2015	Sally Brummitt	31/05/2015		Journal Opening Balance		O/Bal as at 01/06/15	Capital (3000)	0.00	30,000.00	No	No
12	01/06/2015	Sally Brummitt	31/05/2015		Journal Opening Balance		O/Bal as at 01/06/15	Opening Balances Control Account (9998)	0.00	600.00	No	No
12	01/06/2015	Sally Brummitt	31/05/2015		Journal Opening Balance		O/Bal as at 01/06/15	Sales - Men's Footwear (4000)	0.00	79,320.00	No	No
12	01/06/2015	Sally Brummitt	31/05/2015		Journal Opening Balance		O/Bal as at 01/06/15	Sales - Ladies Footwear (4001)	0.00	43,210.00	No	No
12	01/06/2015	Sally Brummitt	31/05/2015		Journal Opening Balance		O/Bal as at 01/06/15	Cash Sales (4002)	0.00	6,798.00	No	No
12	01/06/2015	Sally Brummitt	31/05/2015		Journal Opening Balance		O/Bal as at 01/06/15	Opening Balances Control Account (9998)	0.00	55,432.00	No	No
12	01/06/2015	Sally Brummitt	31/05/2015		Journal Opening Balance		O/Bal as at 01/06/15	Opening Balances Control Account (9998)	0.00	23,410.00	No	No
12	01/06/2015	Sally Brummitt	31/05/2015		Journal Opening Balance		O/Bal as at 01/06/15	Opening Balances Control Account (9998)	0.00	7,231.00	No	No

12	01/06/2015	Sally Brummitt	31/05/2015		Journal Opening Balance		O/Bal as at 01/06/15	Opening Balances Control Account (9998)	0.00	866.00	No	No
12	01/06/2015	Sally Brummitt	31/05/2015		Journal Opening Balance		O/Bal as at 01/06/15	Opening Balances Control Account (9998)	0.00	1,263.00	No	No
12	01/06/2015	Sally Brummitt	31/05/2015		Journal Opening Balance		O/Bal as at 01/06/15	Opening Balances Control Account (9998)	0.00	567.34	No	No
12	01/06/2015	Sally Brummitt	31/05/2015		Journal Opening Balance		O/Bal as at 01/06/15	Opening Balances Control Account (9998)	0.00	830.00	No	No
13	01/06/2015	Sally Brummitt	04/06/2015	Beckers Gate Ltd (SL186)	Sales QE Invoice		1622	Sales - Men's Footwear (4000)	0.00	450.00	No	No
13	01/06/2015	Sally Brummitt	04/06/2015	Beckers Gate Ltd (SL186)	Sales QE Invoice		1622	VAT on Sales (2200)	0.00	90.00	No	No
13	01/06/2015	Sally Brummitt	04/06/2015	Beckers Gate Ltd (SL186)	Sales QE Invoice		1622	Trade Debtors (1100)	540.00	0.00	No	No
14	01/06/2015	Sally Brummitt	06/06/2015	Eaton Bowls Club (SL213)	Sales QE Invoice		1623	Sales - Men's Footwear (4000)	0.00	1,385.00	No	No
14	01/06/2015	Sally Brummitt	06/06/2015	Eaton Bowls Club (SL213)	Sales QE Invoice		1623	VAT on Sales (2200)	0.00	277.00	No	No
14	01/06/2015	Sally Brummitt	06/06/2015	Eaton Bowls Club (SL213)	Sales QE Invoice		1623	Trade Debtors (1100)	1,662.00	0.00	No	No
15	01/06/2015	Sally Brummitt	14/06/2015	Dickens Ladies Footwear (SL307)	Sales QE Invoice		1624	Sales - Men's Footwear (4000)	0.00	450.00	No	No

15	01/06/2015	Sally Brummitt	14/06/2015	Dickens Ladies Footwear (SL307)	Sales QE Invoice		1624	VAT on Sales (2200)	0.00	90.00	No	No
15	01/06/2015	Sally Brummitt	14/06/2015	Dickens Ladies Footwear (SL307)	Sales QE Invoice		1624	Trade Debtors (1100)	540.00	0.00	No	No
16	01/06/2015	Sally Brummitt	14/06/2015	Dickens Ladies Footwear (SL307)	Sales QE Invoice		1624	Sales - Ladies Footwear (4001)	0.00	1,850.00	No	No
16	01/06/2015	Sally Brummitt	14/06/2015	Dickens Ladies Footwear (SL307)	Sales QE Invoice		1624	VAT on Sales (2200)	0.00	370.00	No	No
16	01/06/2015	Sally Brummitt	14/06/2015	Dickens Ladies Footwear (SL307)	Sales QE Invoice		1624	Trade Debtors (1100)	2,220.00	0.00	No	No
17	01/06/2015	Sally Brummitt	17/06/2015	Jones Footwear (SL302)	Sales QE Invoice		1625	Sales - Ladies Footwear (4001)	0.00	1,175.75	No	No
17	01/06/2015	Sally Brummitt	17/06/2015	Jones Footwear (SL302)	Sales QE Invoice		1625	VAT on Sales (2200)	0.00	235.15	No	No
17	01/06/2015	Sally Brummitt	17/06/2015	Jones Footwear (SL302)	Sales QE Invoice		1625	Trade Debtors (1100)	1,410.90	0.00	No	No
18	01/06/2015	Sally Brummitt	08/06/2015	Dickens Ladies Footwear (SL307)	Sales QE Credit		CR10	Trade Debtors (1100)	0.00	282.00	No	No
18	01/06/2015	Sally Brummitt	08/06/2015	Dickens Ladies Footwear (SL307)	Sales QE Credit		CR10	Sales - Ladies Footwear (4001)	235.00	0.00	No	No
18	01/06/2015	Sally Brummitt	08/06/2015	Dickens Ladies Footwear (SL307)	Sales QE Credit		CR10	VAT on Sales (2200)	47.00	0.00	No	No
19	01/06/2015	Sally Brummitt	02/06/2015	Bootsy & Smudge Ltd (PL112)	Purchase QE Invoice		B/752	Purchases - Ladies Footwear (5001)	300.00	0.00	No	No

15	01/06/2015	Sally Brummitt	14/06/2015	Dickens Ladies Footwear (SL307)	Sales QE Invoice		1624	VAT on Sales (2200)	0.00	90.00	No	No
15	01/06/2015	Sally Brummitt	14/06/2015	Dickens Ladies Footwear (SL307)	Sales QE Invoice		1624	Trade Debtors (1100)	540.00	0.00	No	No
16	01/06/2015	Sally Brummitt	14/06/2015	Dickens Ladies Footwear (SL307)	Sales QE Invoice		1624	Sales - Ladies Footwear (4001)	0.00	1,850.00	No	No
16	01/06/2015	Sally Brummitt	14/06/2015	Dickens Ladies Footwear (SL307)	Sales QE Invoice		1624	VAT on Sales (2200)	0.00	370.00	No	No
16	01/06/2015	Sally Brummitt	14/06/2015	Dickens Ladies Footwear (SL307)	Sales QE Invoice		1624	Trade Debtors (1100)	2,220.00	0.00	No	No
17	01/06/2015	Sally Brummitt	17/06/2015	Jones Footwear (SL302)	Sales QE Invoice		1625	Sales - Ladies Footwear (4001)	0.00	1,175.75	No	No
17	01/06/2015	Sally Brummitt	17/06/2015	Jones Footwear (SL302)	Sales QE Invoice		1625	VAT on Sales (2200)	0.00	235.15	No	No
17	01/06/2015	Sally Brummitt	17/06/2015	Jones Footwear (SL302)	Sales QE Invoice		1625	Trade Debtors (1100)	1,410.90	0.00	No	No
18	01/06/2015	Sally Brummitt	08/06/2015	Dickens Ladies Footwear (SL307)	Sales QE Credit		CR10	Trade Debtors (1100)	0.00	282.00	No	No
18	01/06/2015	Sally Brummitt	08/06/2015	Dickens Ladies Footwear (SL307)	Sales QE Credit		CR10	Sales - Ladies Footwear (4001)	235.00	0.00	No	No
18	01/06/2015	Sally Brummitt	08/06/2015	Dickens Ladies Footwear (SL307)	Sales QE Credit		CR10	VAT on Sales (2200)	47.00	0.00	No	No
19	01/06/2015	Sally Brummitt	02/06/2015	Bootsy & Smudge Ltd (PL112)	Purchase QE Invoice		B/752	Purchases - Ladies Footwear (5001)	300.00	0.00	No	No

Mon 01 Jun 2015, 12:46

Page 7 of 12

19	01/06/2015	Sally Brummitt	02/06/2015	Bootsy & Smudge Ltd (PL112)	Purchase QE Invoice	B/752	VAT on Purchases (2201)	60.00	0.00	No	No
19	01/06/2015	Sally Brummitt	02/06/2015	Bootsy & Smudge Ltd (PL112)	Purchase QE Invoice	B/752	Trade Creditors (2100)	0.00	360.00	No	No
20	01/06/2015	Sally Brummitt	10/06/2015	Briggsthorpe Boots (PL168)	Purchase QE Invoice	12350	Purchases - Men's Footwear (5000)	2,500.00	0.00	No	No
20	01/06/2015	Sally Brummitt	10/06/2015	Briggsthorpe Boots (PL168)	Purchase QE Invoice	12350	VAT on Purchases (2201)	500.00	0.00	No	No
20	01/06/2015	Sally Brummitt	10/06/2015	Briggsthorpe Boots (PL168)	Purchase QE Invoice	12350	Trade Creditors (2100)	0.00	3,000.00	No	No
21	01/06/2015	Sally Brummitt	10/06/2015	Gallows Fashion (PL172)	Purchase QE Invoice	G-2285	Purchases - Men's Footwear (5000)	2,500.00	0.00	No	No
21	01/06/2015	Sally Brummitt	10/06/2015	Gallows Fashion (PL172)	Purchase QE Invoice	G-2285	VAT on Purchases (2201)	500.00	0.00	No	No
21	01/06/2015	Sally Brummitt	10/06/2015	Gallows Fashion (PL172)	Purchase QE Invoice	G-2285	Trade Creditors (2100)	0.00	3,000.00	No	No
22	01/06/2015	Sally Brummitt	13/06/2015	Bootsy & Smudge Ltd (PL112)	Purchase QE Invoice	B/753	Purchases - Men's Footwear (5000)	200.00	0.00	No	Yes
22	01/06/2015	Sally Brummitt	13/06/2015	Bootsy & Smudge Ltd (PL112)	Purchase QE Invoice	B/753	VAT on Purchases (2201)	40.00	0.00	No	Yes
22	01/06/2015	Sally Brummitt	13/06/2015	Bootsy & Smudge Ltd (PL112)	Purchase QE Invoice	B/753	Trade Creditors (2100)	0.00	240.00	No	Yes
22	01/06/2015	Sally Brummitt	13/06/2015	Bootsy & Smudge Ltd (PL112)	Purchase QE Invoice	B/753	Purchases - Men's Footwear (5000)	0.00	200.00	No	Yes
22	01/06/2015	Sally Brummitt	13/06/2015	Bootsy & Smudge Ltd (PL112)	Purchase QE Invoice	B/753	VAT on Purchases (2201)	0.00	40.00	No	Yes
22	01/06/2015	Sally Brummitt	13/06/2015	Bootsy & Smudge Ltd (PL112)	Purchase QE Invoice	B/753	Trade Creditors (2100)	240.00	0.00	No	Yes

23	01/06/2015	Sally Brummitt	11/06/2015	Beckers Gate Ltd (SL186)	Customer Receipt	Chq No. 199846	Current (1200)	4,811.88	0.00	Yes	No
23	01/06/2015	Sally Brummitt	11/06/2015	Beckers Gate Ltd (SL186)	Customer Receipt	Chq No. 199846	Trade Debtors (1100)	0.00	4,811.88	No	No
24	01/06/2015	Sally Brummitt	14/06/2015	Eaton Bowls Club (SL213)	Customer Receipt	Chq No. 107654	Current (1200)	961.98	0.00	No	Yes
24	01/06/2015	Sally Brummitt	14/06/2015	Eaton Bowls Club (SL213)	Customer Receipt	Chq No. 107654	Trade Debtors (1100)	0.00	961.98	No	Yes
24	01/06/2015	Sally Brummitt	14/06/2015	Eaton Bowls Club (SL213)	Customer Receipt	Chq No. 107654	Current (1200)	0.00	961.98	No	Yes
24	01/06/2015	Sally Brummitt	14/06/2015	Eaton Bowls Club (SL213)	Customer Receipt	Chq No. 107654	Trade Debtors (1100)	961.98	0.00	No	Yes
25	01/06/2015	Sally Brummitt	14/06/2015	Jones Footwear (SL302)	Customer Receipt	Chq No.244536	Current (1200)	3,828.75	0.00	Yes	No
25	01/06/2015	Sally Brummitt	14/06/2015	Jones Footwear (SL302)	Customer Receipt	Chq No.244536	Trade Debtors (1100)	0.00	3,828.75	No	No
26	01/06/2015	Sally Brummitt	18/06/2015	Gallows Fashion (PL172)	Supplier Payment	Chq No. 109887	Trade Creditors (2100)	400.00	0.00	No	No
26	01/06/2015	Sally Brummitt	18/06/2015	Gallows Fashion (PL172)	Supplier Payment	Chq No. 109887	Current (1200)	0.00	400.00	No	No
27	01/06/2015	Sally Brummitt	18/06/2015	Briggsthorpe Boots (PL168)	Supplier Payment	Chq No. 109888	Trade Creditors (2100)	23,300.00	0.00	No	No
27	01/06/2015	Sally Brummitt	18/06/2015	Briggsthorpe Boots (PL168)	Supplier Payment	Chq No. 109888	Current (1200)	0.00	23,300.00	Yes	No
28	01/06/2015	Sally Brummitt	05/06/2015		Other Payment	PCV 010	Cash in Hand (1210)	0.00	9.90	No	No
28	01/06/2015	Sally Brummitt	05/06/2015		Other Payment	PCV 010	Refreshment (7502)	9.90	0.00	No	No
29	01/06/2015	Sally Brummitt	10/06/2015		Other Payment	PCV 011	Cash in Hand (1210)	0.00	13.50	No	No
29	01/06/2015	Sally Brummitt	10/06/2015		Other Payment	PCV 011	Office Stationery (7501)	11.25	0.00	No	No

29	01/06/2015	Sally Brummitt	10/06/2015		Other Payment	PCV 011	VAT on Purchases (2201)	2.25	0.00	No	No
30	01/06/2015	Sally Brummitt	10/06/2015		Bank Transfer	TRF02	Current (1200)	0.00	23.40	Yes	No
30	01/06/2015	Sally Brummitt	10/06/2015		Bank Transfer	TRF02	Cash in Hand (1210)	23.40	0.00	No	No
31	01/06/2015	Sally Brummitt	23/06/2015		Other Receipt	F027	Sales - Men's Footwear (4000)	0.00	64.66	No	No
31	01/06/2015	Sally Brummitt	23/06/2015		Other Receipt	F027	VAT on Sales (2200)	0.00	12.93	No	No
31	01/06/2015	Sally Brummitt	23/06/2015		Other Receipt	F027	Current (1200)	77.59	0.00	Yes	No
32	01/06/2015	Sally Brummitt	13/06/2015	Bootsy & Smudge Ltd (PL112)	Purchase QE Invoice	B/753	Purchases - Ladies Footwear (5001)	200.00	0.00	No	No
32	01/06/2015	Sally Brummitt	13/06/2015	Bootsy & Smudge Ltd (PL112)	Purchase QE Invoice	B/753	VAT on Purchases (2201)	40.00	0.00	No	No
32	01/06/2015	Sally Brummitt	13/06/2015	Bootsy & Smudge Ltd (PL112)	Purchase QE Invoice	B/753	Trade Creditors (2100)	0.00	240.00	No	No
33	01/06/2015	Sally Brummitt	25/06/2015		Other Payment	Quarterly Standing Order	Current (1200)	0.00	193.00	No	Yes
33	01/06/2015	Sally Brummitt	25/06/2015		Other Payment	Quarterly Standing Order	Electricity (7200)	193.00	0.00	No	Yes
33	01/06/2015	Sally Brummitt	25/06/2015		Other Payment	Quarterly Standing Order	VAT on Purchases (2201)	0.00	0.00	No	Yes
33	01/06/2015	Sally Brummitt	25/06/2015		Other Payment	Quarterly Standing Order	Current (1200)	193.00	0.00	No	Yes
33	01/06/2015	Sally Brummitt	25/06/2015		Other Payment	Quarterly Standing Order	Electricity (7200)	0.00	193.00	No	Yes
33	01/06/2015	Sally Brummitt	25/06/2015		Other Payment	Quarterly Standing Order	VAT on Purchases (2201)	0.00	0.00	No	Yes
34	01/06/2015	Sally Brummitt	25/06/2015		Other Payment	Quarterly Standing Order	Current (1200)	0.00	193.00	Yes	No

34	01/06/2015	Sally Brummitt	25/06/2015		Other Payment	Quarterly Standing Order	Electricity (7200)	193.00	0.00	No	No
34	01/06/2015	Sally Brummitt	25/06/2015		Other Payment	Quarterly Standing Order	VAT on Purchases (2201)	0.00	0.00	No	No
35	01/06/2015	Sally Brummitt	30/06/2015		Other Receipt	Quarterly Standing Order	Rent Income (4900)	0.00	1,500.00	No	Yes
35	01/06/2015	Sally Brummitt	30/06/2015		Other Receipt	Quarterly Standing Order	Current (1200)	1,500.00	0.00	No	Yes
35	01/06/2015	Sally Brummitt	30/06/2015		Other Receipt	Quarterly Standing Order	Rent Income (4900)	1,500.00	0.00	No	Yes
35	01/06/2015	Sally Brummitt	30/06/2015		Other Receipt	Quarterly Standing Order	Current (1200)	0.00	1,500.00	No	Yes
36	01/06/2015	Sally Brummitt	30/06/2015		Other Receipt	Quarterly Standing Order	Rent Income (4900)	0.00	1,500.00	No	No
36	01/06/2015	Sally Brummitt	30/06/2015		Other Receipt	Quarterly Standing Order	Current (1200)	1,500.00	0.00	Yes	No
37	01/06/2015	Sally Brummitt	25/06/2015		Journal	Journal No: 209	Drawings (3260)	3,200.00	0.00	No	No
37	01/06/2015	Sally Brummitt	25/06/2015		Journal	Journal No: 209	Current (1200)	0.00	3,200.00	Yes	No
38	01/06/2015	Sally Brummitt	22/06/2015		Other Receipt	DC03	Sales - Ladies Footwear (4001)	0.00	45.00	No	No
38	01/06/2015	Sally Brummitt	22/06/2015		Other Receipt	DC03	VAT on Sales (2200)	0.00	9.00	No	No
38	01/06/2015	Sally Brummitt	22/06/2015		Other Receipt	DC03	Current (1200)	54.00	0.00	Yes	No
39	01/06/2015	Sally Brummitt	14/06/2015	Eaton Bowls Club (SL213)	Customer Receipt	Chq No. 107654	Current (1200)	961.98	0.00	Yes	No
39	01/06/2015	Sally Brummitt	14/06/2015	Eaton Bowls Club (SL213)	Customer Receipt	Chq No. 107654	Trade Debtors (1100)	0.00	961.98	No	No
40	01/06/2015	Sally Brummitt	14/06/2015	Eaton Bowls Club (SL213)	Customer Refund	Bounced Cheque	Trade Debtors (1100)	961.98	0.00	No	No

40	01/06/2015	Sally Brummitt	14/06/2015	Eaton Bowls Club (SL213)	Customer Refund		Bounced Cheque	Current (1200)	0.00	961.98	Yes	No
41	01/06/2015	Sally Brummitt	30/06/2015	Eaton Bowls Club (SL213)	Sales QE Credit		Write off	Trade Debtors (1100)	0.00	961.98	No	No
41	01/06/2015	Sally Brummitt	30/06/2015	Eaton Bowls Club (SL213)	Sales QE Credit		Write off	Bad Debts (8100)	961.98	0.00	No	No
42	01/06/2015	Sally Brummitt	30/06/2015		Bank Payment		Bank Charge	Current (1200)	0.00	50.00	Yes	No
42	01/06/2015	Sally Brummitt	30/06/2015		Bank Payment		Bank Charge	Bank charges and interest (7900)	50.00	0.00	No	No
43	01/06/2015	Sally Brummitt	30/06/2015	Eaton Bowls Club (SL213)	Sales QE Credit		Write off	Trade Debtors (1100)	0.00	1,662.00	No	No
43	01/06/2015	Sally Brummitt	30/06/2015	Eaton Bowls Club (SL213)	Sales QE Credit		Write off	Bad Debts (8100)	1,662.00	0.00	No	No

TASK 17

Nominal Ledger Activity Report for Trade Creditors and Sales – Ladies Footwear

Shoes 4U

Detailed Nominal Activity: Trade Creditors (2100)

31 May, 2015 - 30 June, 2015

Transaction Type: All

Transaction number	Date	Invoice Number	Name	Type	Reference	Description	Debit	Credit
5	31/05/2015		Bootsy & Smudge Ltd (PL112)	Supplier OB Invoice	B/468	Inv B/468 - 22/05/15		2,881.26
6	31/05/2015		Briggsthorpe Boots (PL168)	Supplier OB Invoice	0001087	Inv 0001087 - 18/05/15		43,200.00
7	31/05/2015		Gallows Fashion (PL172)	Supplier OB Invoice	G-01239	Inv G-01239 - 16/05/15		400.00
8	31/05/2015		Dickens Ladies Footwear (PL173)	Supplier OB Invoice	06345	Inv 06345 - 16/05/15		567.00
19	02/06/2015		Bootsy & Smudge Ltd (PL112)	Purchase QE Invoice	B/752			360.00
20	10/06/2015		Briggsthorpe Boots (PL168)	Purchase QE Invoice	12350			3,000.00
21	10/06/2015		Gallows Fashion (PL172)	Purchase QE Invoice	G-2285			3,000.00
32	13/06/2015		Bootsy & Smudge Ltd (PL112)	Purchase QE Invoice	B/753			240.00
26	18/06/2015		Gallows Fashion (PL172)	Supplier Payment	Chq No. 109887		400.00	
27	18/06/2015		Briggsthorpe Boots (PL168)	Supplier Payment	Chq No. 109888		23,300.00	

Shoes 4U

Detailed Nominal Activity: Sales - Ladies Footwear (4001)

31 May, 2015 - 30 June, 2015

Transaction Type: All

Transaction number	Date	Invoice Number	Name	Type	Reference	Description	Debit	Credit
12	31/05/2015			Journal Opening Balance	O/Bal as at 01/06/15	(Opening Balance)		43,210.00
18	08/06/2015		Dickens Ladies Footwear (SL307)	Sales QE Credit	CR10	Damaged in transit	235.00	
16	14/06/2015		Dickens Ladies Footwear (SL307)	Sales QE Invoice	1624			1,850.00
17	17/06/2015		Jones Footwear (SL302)	Sales QE Invoice	1625			1,175.75
38	22/06/2015			Other Receipt	DC03			45.00

TASK 17

Aged Debtors Analysis

Shoes 4U

Aged Debtors Breakdown

To Date: 30/06/2015

Customer	Date	Reference	Total	O/S Amt	< 30 days	< 60 days	< 90 days	< 120 days	Older
Beckers Gate Ltd (SL186) Credit limit: £5,000.00 Terms: 30 days									
	04/06/2015	QE-1622	540.00	540.00	540.00				
			£540.00	**£540.00**	**£0.00**	**£0.00**	**£0.00**	**£0.00**	
Dickens Ladies Footwear (SL307) Credit limit: £11,000.00 Terms: 30 days									
	31/05/2015	OB-1601	783.66	783.66		783.66			
	14/06/2015	QE-1624	540.00	540.00	540.00				
	14/06/2015	QE-1624	2,220.00	2,220.00	2,220.00				
	08/06/2015	QE-CR10	-282.00	-282.00	-282.00				
			£3,261.66	**£2,478.00**	**£783.66**	**£0.00**	**£0.00**	**£0.00**	
Eaton Bowls Club (SL213) Credit limit: £3,000.00 Terms: 30 days									
	31/05/2015	OB-1582	961.98	961.98		961.98			
	06/06/2015	QE-1623	1,662.00	1,662.00	1,662.00				
	30/06/2015	QE-Write off	-961.98	-961.98	-961.98				
	30/06/2015	QE-Write off	-1,662.00	-1,662.00	-1,662.00				
				£0.00	**-£961.98**	**£961.98**	**£0.00**	**£0.00**	**£0.00**
Jones Footwear (SL302) Credit limit: £8,000.00 Terms: 30 days									
	17/06/2015	QE-1625	1,410.90	1,410.90	1,410.90				
				£1,410.90	**£1,410.90**	**£0.00**	**£0.00**	**£0.00**	**£0.00**
		TOTAL		**£5,212.56**	**£3,466.92**	**£1,745.64**	**£0.00**	**£0.00**	**£0.00**

PRACTICE PAPER 4

SPORTS GEAR ANSWERS

TASK 3.2

Customer Address List

Sports Gear

Customer Address List

Address Types: All

Customer Name	Address	Contact name	Phone	Mobile	Email	Fax
J Hollingham (SL01)	56 Glencoe Avenue Gants Hill Ilford Essex IG1 6FR United Kingdom	Main Contact				
Paul McCallum (SL02)	34 St Albans Road Seven Kings Essex IG7 8DS United Kingdom	Main Contact				
Kerry Jenkins (SL03)	34 Gloucester Road Gillingham Kent ME14 3TL United Kingdom	Main Contact				
Harry Bucket (SL04)	54 Dale Road Harrogate North Yorks Y02 3HN United Kingdom	Main Contact				
Evelyn Rose (SL05)	98 Crabtree Drive Bromley Kent DA3 6AY United Kingdom	Main Contact				

TASK 3.2

Supplier Address List

Sports Gear

Supplier Address List

Address Types: All

Supplier Name	Address	Contact name	Phone	Mobile	Email	Fax
Radcliff and Sons (PL01)	Orient House Lower Clapham London E1 2RH United Kingdom	Main Contact				
Tennison Bros (PL02)	White Cottage London WC1 6YD United Kingdom	Main Contact				
Skipton & Co (PL03)	22 Chatworths Lane Water Square London EC1V 6NJ United Kingdom	Main Contact				
Evelyn Rose (PL04)	98 Crabtree Drive Bromley Kent DA3 6AY United Kingdom	Main Contact				

TASK 3.2

Trial Balance

Sports Gear

Trial Balance Report

From Date: 31/05/2015   To Date: 30/06/2015

Nominal Code	Name	Debits	Credits
0030	Office equipment - Cost	8,430.00	
0040	Furniture and Fixtures - Cost	18,000.00	
0050	Motor Vehicles - Cost	15,500.00	
1100	Trade Debtors	8,445.46	
1200	Current	3,325.40	
1210	Cash In Hand	300.00	
2100	Trade Creditors		8,914.14
2200	VAT on Sales		3,458.00
2201	VAT on Purchases	1,120.00	
3000	Capital		52,000.00
3260	Drawings	1,294.00	
4000	Sales - Tennis Racquets		13,266.78
4001	Sales - Exercise Bikes		22,310.00
4002	Sales - Golf Clubs		9,543.00
4003	Sales - Fishing Rods		5,644.00
5000	Purchases - Tennis Racquets	21,354.00	
5001	Purchases - Exercise Bikes	25,610.00	
5002	Purchases - Golf Clubs	5,475.00	
5003	Purchases - Fishing Rods	4,796.00	
7200	Electricity	496.06	
7500	Office Stationery	430.00	
7501	Postage	560.00	

	TOTAL	£115,135.92	£115,135.92

TASK 11

Trial Balance

Sports Gear

Trial Balance Report

From Date: 30/06/2015   To Date: 31/07/2015

Nominal Code	Name	Debits	Credits
0030	Office equipment - Cost	8,430.00	
0040	Furniture and Fixtures - Cost	18,000.00	
0050	Motor Vehicles - Cost	15,500.00	
1100	Trade Debtors	6,108.50	
1200	Current	6,811.61	
1210	Cash In Hand		132.16
2100	Trade Creditors		3,629.46
2200	VAT on Sales		5,010.07
2201	VAT on Purchases	1,662.62	
3000	Capital		52,000.00
3260	Drawings	1,294.00	
4000	Sales - Tennis Racquets		16,276.83
4001	Sales - Exercise Bikes		25,222.47
4002	Sales - Golf Clubs		11,056.80
4003	Sales - Fishing Rods		5,968.00
5000	Purchases - Tennis Racquets	21,904.00	
5001	Purchases - Exercise Bikes	25,930.00	
5002	Purchases - Golf Clubs	6,303.55	
5003	Purchases - Fishing Rods	5,467.00	
7200	Electricity	496.06	
7500	Office Stationery	449.90	
7501	Postage	938.55	
	TOTAL	**£119,295.79**	**£119,295.79**

TASK 11

Sales Day Book

Sports Gear

Sales Day Book Report

From Date: 30/06/2015

To Date: 31/07/2015

Type: Sales QE Invoice

Trans ID	Type	Date	Name	Invoice Number	Ref	Details	Net	VAT	Total
13	Sales QE Invoice	04/07/2015	J Hollingham		1052	20 Tennis Racquets	882.00	176.40	1,058.40
14	Sales QE Invoice	04/07/2015	J Hollingham		1052	10 Exercise Bikes	1,023.60	204.72	1,228.32
15	Sales QE Invoice	04/07/2015	J Hollingham		1052	6 Fishing Rods	324.00	64.80	388.80
16	Sales QE Invoice	06/07/2015	Kerry Jenkins		1053	3 Tennis Racquets	132.30	26.46	158.76
17	Sales QE Invoice	08/07/2015	Harry Bucket		1054	18 Golf Clubs	1,513.80	302.76	1,816.56
						TOTAL	£3,875.70	£775.14	£4,650.84

TASK 11

Purchase Day Book

Sports Gear

Purchase Day Book Report

From Date: 30/06/2015

To Date: 31/07/2015

Type: Purchase QE Invoice

Trans ID	Type	Date	Name	Invoice Number	Ref	Details	Net	VAT	Total
19	Purchase QE Invoice	03/07/2015	Radcliff and Sons		1099		550.00	110.00	660.00
20	Purchase QE Invoice	05/07/2015	Tennison Bros		B-1147		320.00	64.00	384.00
21	Purchase QE Invoice	05/07/2015	Tennison Bros		B-1147		35.00	0.00	35.00
22	Purchase QE Invoice	10/07/2015	Skipton & Co		2785		938.00	187.60	1,125.60
23	Purchase QE Invoice	10/07/2015	Evelyn Rose		A/5698		671.00	134.20	805.20
						TOTAL	£2,514.00	£495.80	£3,009.80

TASK 11

Customer Activity Report

Sports Gear

Customer Activity Report

From Date: 30/06/2015

To Date: 31/07/2015

J Hollingham (SL01)

Date	Number	Reference	Type	Net	VAT	Total	Discount	Outstanding
30/06/2015		1001	Customer OB Invoice	3,462.12	0.00	3,462.12		0.00
04/07/2015		1052	Sales QE Invoice	882.00	176.40	1,058.40		1,058.40
04/07/2015		1052	Sales QE Invoice	1,023.60	204.72	1,228.32		1,228.32
04/07/2015		1052	Sales QE Invoice	324.00	64.80	388.80		388.80
17/07/2015		CR34	Sales QE Credit	-510.63	-102.12	-612.75		0.00
19/07/2015		Chq No. 542321	Customer Receipt			-2,849.37	0.00	0.00
						2,675.52		**2,675.52**

Paul McCallum (SL02)

Date	Number	Reference	Type	Net	VAT	Total	Discount	Outstanding
30/06/2015		0087	Customer OB Invoice	514.68	0.00	514.68		514.68
						514.68		**514.68**

Kerry Jenkins (SL03)

Date	Number	Reference	Type	Net	VAT	Total	Discount	Outstanding
30/06/2015		0093	Customer OB Invoice	758.34	0.00	758.34		0.00
06/07/2015		1053	Sales QE Invoice	132.30	26.46	158.76		158.76
12/07/2015		Chq No. 222547	Customer Receipt			-758.34	0.00	0.00
						158.76		**158.76**

Harry Bucket (SL04)

Date	Number	Reference	Type	Net	VAT	Total	Discount	Outstanding
30/06/2015		1003	Customer OB Invoice	2,767.34	0.00	2,767.34		0.00
08/07/2015		1054	Sales QE Invoice	1,513.80	302.76	1,816.56		1,816.56
13/07/2015		BACS	Customer Receipt			-2,767.34	0.00	0.00
						1,816.56		**1,816.56**

Evelyn Rose (SL05)

Date	Number	Reference	Type	Net	VAT	Total	Discount	Outstanding
30/06/2015		1004	Customer OB Invoice	942.98	0.00	942.98		942.98
						942.98		**942.98**

TASK 11

Supplier Activity Report

Sports Gear

Supplier Activity Report

From Date: 30/06/2015

To Date: 31/07/2015

Radcliff and Sons (PL01)

Date	Number	Reference	Type	Net	VAT	Total	Discount	Outstanding
30/06/2015	1874		Supplier OB Invoice	5,362.14	0.00	5,362.14		0.00
03/07/2015	1099		Purchase QE Invoice	550.00	110.00	660.00		660.00
14/07/2015		Chq No. 170012	Supplier Payment			-5,362.14	0.00	0.00
						660.00		660.00

Tennison Bros (PL02)

Date	Number	Reference	Type	Net	VAT	Total	Discount	Outstanding
30/06/2015		B-321	Supplier OB Invoice	2,801.00	0.00	2,801.00		0.00
05/07/2015		B-1147	Purchase QE Invoice	320.00	64.00	384.00		384.00
05/07/2015		B-1147	Purchase QE Invoice	35.00	0.00	35.00		35.00
17/07/2015		Chq No. 170013	Supplier Payment			-2,801.00	0.00	0.00
						419.00		419.00

Skipton & Co (PL03)

Date	Number	Reference	Type	Net	VAT	Total	Discount	Outstanding
30/06/2015		1087	Supplier OB Invoice	501.00	0.00	501.00		501.00
10/07/2015		2785	Purchase QE Invoice	938.00	187.60	1,125.60		1,125.60
19/07/2015		CX432	Purchase QE Credit	-109.45	-21.89	-131.34		-131.34
						1,495.26		1,495.26

Evelyn Rose (PL04)

Date	Number	Reference	Type	Net	VAT	Total	Discount	Outstanding
30/06/2015		A193	Supplier OB Invoice	250.00	0.00	250.00		250.00
10/07/2015		A/5698	Purchase QE Invoice	671.00	134.20	805.20		805.20
						1,055.20		1,055.20

TASK 11

Aged Creditors Report

Sports Gear

Aged Creditors Breakdown

To Date: 31/07/2015

Supplier	Date	Reference	Total	O/S Amt	< 30 days	< 60 days	< 90 days	< 120 days	Older
Evelyn Rose (PL04) Credit limit: £3,000.00 Terms: 30 days									
	10/07/2015	A/5698	805.20	805.20	805.20				
	30/06/2015	A193	250.00	250.00		250.00			
			£1,055.20	£805.20	£250.00	£0.00	£0.00	£0.00	
Radcliff and Sons (PL01) Credit limit: £15,500.00 Terms: 30 days									
	03/07/2015	1099	660.00	660.00	660.00				
			£660.00	£660.00	£0.00	£0.00	£0.00	£0.00	£0.00
Skipton & Co (PL03) Credit limit: £9,000.00 Terms: 30 days									
	30/06/2015	1087	501.00	501.00		501.00			
	10/07/2015	2785	1,125.60	1,125.60	1,125.60				
	19/07/2015	CX432	-131.34	-131.34	-131.34				
			£1,495.26	£994.26	£501.00	£0.00	£0.00	£0.00	
Tennison Bros (PL02) Credit limit: £11,000.00 Terms: 30 days									
	05/07/2015	B-1147	384.00	384.00	384.00				
	05/07/2015	B-1147	35.00	35.00	35.00				
			£419.00	£419.00	£0.00	£0.00	£0.00	£0.00	
		TOTAL	£3,629.46	£2,878.46	£751.00	£0.00	£0.00	£0.00	

TASK 11

Aged Debtors Report

Sports Gear

Aged Debtors Breakdown

To Date: 31/07/2015

Customer	Date	Reference	Total	O/S Amt	< 30 days	< 60 days	< 90 days	< 120 days	Older
Evelyn Rose (SL05) Credit limit: £7,000.00 Terms: 30 days									
	30/06/2015	OB-1004	942.98	942.98		942.98			
			£942.98	**£0.00**	**£942.98**	**£0.00**	**£0.00**	**£0.00**	
Harry Bucket (SL04) Credit limit: £12,000.00 Terms: 30 days									
	08/07/2015	QE-1054	1,816.56	1,816.56	1,816.56				
			£1,816.56	**£1,816.56**	**£0.00**	**£0.00**	**£0.00**	**£0.00**	
J Hollingham (SL01) Credit limit: £5,000.00 Terms: 30 days									
	04/07/2015	QE-1052	1,058.40	1,058.40	1,058.40				
	04/07/2015	QE-1052	1,228.32	1,228.32	1,228.32				
	04/07/2015	QE-1052	388.80	388.80	388.80				
			£2,675.52	**£2,675.52**	**£0.00**	**£0.00**	**£0.00**	**£0.00**	
Kerry Jenkins (SL03) Credit limit: £8,000.00 Terms: 30 days									
	06/07/2015	QE-1053	158.76	158.76	158.76				
			£158.76	**£158.76**	**£0.00**	**£0.00**	**£0.00**	**£0.00**	
Paul McCallum (SL02) Credit limit: £9,500.00 Terms: 30 days									
	30/06/2015	OB-0087	514.68	514.68		514.68			
			£514.68	**£0.00**	**£514.68**	**£0.00**	**£0.00**	**£0.00**	
		TOTAL	**£6,108.50**	**£4,650.84**	**£1,457.66**	**£0.00**	**£0.00**	**£0.00**	

TASK 11

Customer Statement

Sports Gear

Statement Summary Report

Statement period 30/06/2015 to 31/07/2015

Paul McCallum (SL02)
34 St Albans Road
Seven Kings
Essex
IG7 8DS
United Kingdom

Date	Activity	Invoices	Payments	Balance
30/06/2015	Sales Invoice	514.68	0.00	514.68

Summary				
Balance Owed (£) At 31/07/2015				514.68

TASK 23

Customer Address List

Sports Gear

Customer Address List

Address Types: All

Customer Name	Address	Contact name	Phone	Mobile	Email	Fax
J Hollingham (SL01)	56 Glencoe Avenue Gants Hill Illford Essex IG1 6FR United Kingdom	Main Contact				
Paul McCallum (SL02)	34 St Albans Road Seven Kings Essex IG7 8DS United Kingdom	Main Contact				
Kerry Jenkins (SL03)	34 Gloucester Road Gillingham Kent ME14 3TL United Kingdom	Main Contact				
Harry Bucket (SL04)	137 Chester Road Capel Corner CR3 2SA United Kingdom	Main Contact	08459 754 256			
Evelyn Rose (SL05)	98 Crabtree Drive Bromley Kent DA3 6AY United Kingdom	Main Contact				

TASK 23

Customer Activity (detailed report)

Sports Gear

Customer Activity Report

From Date: 30/06/2015

To Date: 31/07/2015

J Hollingham (SL01)

Date	Number	Reference	Type	Net	VAT	Total	Discount	Outstanding
30/06/2015		1001	Customer OB Invoice	3,462.12	0.00	3,462.12		0.00
04/07/2015		1052	Sales QE Invoice	882.00	176.40	1,058.40		0.00
04/07/2015		1052	Sales QE Invoice	1,023.60	204.72	1,228.32		0.00
04/07/2015		1052	Sales QE Invoice	324.00	64.80	388.80		0.00
17/07/2015		CR34	Sales QE Credit	-510.63	-102.12	-612.75		0.00
19/07/2015		Chq No. 542321	Customer Receipt			-2,849.37	0.00	0.00
28/07/2015		Chq No. 087651	Customer Receipt			-2,675.52	0.00	0.00
						0.00		**0.00**

Paul McCallum (SL02)

Date	Number	Reference	Type	Net	VAT	Total	Discount	Outstanding
30/06/2015		0087	Customer OB Invoice	514.68	0.00	514.68		514.68
31/07/2015		Write Off	Sales QE Credit	-514.68	0.00	-514.68		-514.68
						0.00		**0.00**

Kerry Jenkins (SL03)

Date	Number	Reference	Type	Net	VAT	Total	Discount	Outstanding
30/06/2015		0093	Customer OB Invoice	758.34	0.00	758.34		758.34
06/07/2015		1053	Sales QE Invoice	132.30	26.46	158.76		158.76
12/07/2015		Chq No. 222547	Customer Receipt			-758.34		0.00
12/07/2015		Bounced Cheque	Customer Refund			758.34		0.00
						917.10		**917.10**

Harry Bucket (SL04)

Date	Number	Reference	Type	Net	VAT	Total	Discount	Outstanding
30/06/2015		1003	Customer OB Invoice	2,767.34	0.00	2,767.34		0.00
08/07/2015		1054	Sales QE Invoice	1,513.80	302.76	1,816.56		1,316.56
13/07/2015		BACS	Customer Receipt			-2,767.34	0.00	0.00
28/07/2015		Chq No. 198871	Customer Receipt			-500.00	0.00	0.00
						1,316.56		**1,316.56**

Evelyn Rose (SL05)

Date	Number	Reference	Type	Net	VAT	Total	Discount	Outstanding
30/06/2015		1004	Customer OB Invoice	942.98	0.00	942.98		942.98
						942.98		**942.98**

TASK 23

Supplier Activity (detailed report)

Sports Gear

Supplier Activity Report

From Date: 30/06/2015

To Date: 31/07/2015

Radcliff and Sons (PL01)

Date	Number	Reference	Type	Net	VAT	Total	Discount	Outstanding
30/06/2015		1874	Supplier OB Invoice	5,362.14	0.00	5,362.14		0.00
03/07/2015		1099	Purchase QE Invoice	550.00	110.00	660.00		0.00
14/07/2015		Chq No. 170012	Supplier Payment			-5,362.14	0.00	0.00
28/07/2015		Chq No. 170015	Supplier Payment			-660.00	0.00	0.00
						0.00		0.00

Tennison Bros (PL02)

Date	Number	Reference	Type	Net	VAT	Total	Discount	Outstanding
30/06/2015		B-321	Supplier OB Invoice	2,801.00	0.00	2,801.00		0.00
05/07/2015		B-1147	Purchase QE Invoice	320.00	64.00	384.00		384.00
05/07/2015		B-1147	Purchase QE Invoice	35.00	0.00	35.00		35.00
17/07/2015		Chq No. 170013	Supplier Payment			-2,801.00	0.00	0.00
						419.00		419.00

Skipton & Co (PL03)

Date	Number	Reference	Type	Net	VAT	Total	Discount	Outstanding
30/06/2015		1087	Supplier OB Invoice	501.00	0.00	501.00		501.00
10/07/2015		2785	Purchase QE Invoice	938.00	187.60	1,125.60		1,125.60
19/07/2015		CX432	Purchase QE Credit	-109.45	-21.89	-131.34		-131.34
28/07/2015		Chq No. 170014	Supplier Payment			-501.00		-501.00
						994.26		994.26

Evelyn Rose (PL04)

Date	Number	Reference	Type	Net	VAT	Total	Discount	Outstanding
30/06/2015		A193	Supplier OB Invoice	250.00	0.00	250.00		250.00
10/07/2015		A/5698	Purchase QE Invoice	671.00	134.20	805.20		805.20
						1,055.20		1,055.20

TASK 23

Trial Balance for July

Sports Gear

Trial Balance Report

From Date: 30/06/2015   To Date: 31/07/2015

Nominal Code	Name	Debits	Credits
0030	Office equipment - Cost	8,430.00	
0040	Furniture and Fixtures - Cost	18,000.00	
0050	Motor Vehicles - Cost	15,500.00	
1100	Trade Debtors	3,176.64	
1200	Current	4,166.44	
1210	Cash in Hand	300.00	
2100	Trade Creditors		2,468.46
2200	VAT on Sales		5,027.40
2201	VAT on Purchases	1,662.62	
3000	Capital		52,000.00
3260	Drawings	4,735.00	
4000	Sales - Tennis Racquets		16,318.50
4001	Sales - Exercise Bikes		25,222.47
4002	Sales - Golf Clubs		11,101.80
4003	Sales - Fishing Rods		5,968.00
5000	Purchases - Tennis Racquets	21,904.00	
5001	Purchases - Exercise Bikes	25,930.00	
5002	Purchases - Golf Clubs	6,303.55	
5003	Purchases - Fishing Rods	5,467.00	
7200	Electricity	496.06	
7500	Office Stationery	449.90	
7501	Postage	938.55	
7610	Insurance	100.00	
7900	Bank charges and interest	32.19	
8100	Bad Debts	514.68	
	TOTAL	**£118,106.63**	**£118,106.63**

TASK 23

Nominal Ledger Activity Report for Bank/Petty Cash

Sports Gear

Detailed Nominal Activity: Current (1200)

30 June, 2015 - 31 July, 2015

Transaction Type: All

Transaction number	Date	Invoice Number	Name	Type	Reference	Description	Debit	Credit
10	30/06/2015			Bank Opening Balance			3,325.40	
43	12/07/2015		Kerry Jenkins (SL03)	Customer Receipt	Chq No. 222547		758.34	
44	12/07/2015		Kerry Jenkins (SL03)	Customer Refund	Bounced Cheque			758.34
32	13/07/2015			Other Receipt	REC101		1,200.00	
27	13/07/2015		Harry Bucket (SL04)	Customer Receipt	BACS		2,767.34	
28	14/07/2015		Radcliff and Sons (PL01)	Supplier Payment	Chq No. 170012			5,362.14
41	14/07/2015			Other Receipt	ST5		50.00	
33	15/07/2015			Other Receipt	REC102		2,879.40	
34	15/07/2015			Other Receipt	REC103		1,194.90	
29	17/07/2015		Tennison Bros (PL02)	Supplier Payment	Chq No. 170013			2,801.00
42	19/07/2015			Other Receipt	CS03		54.00	
25	19/07/2015		J Hollingham (SL01)	Customer Receipt	Chq No. 542321		2,849.37	
36	25/07/2015			Journal	JNL004	Drawings		3,441.00
37	28/07/2015		Skipton & Co (PL03)	Supplier Payment	Chq No. 170014			501.00
46	28/07/2015			Other Payment	Monthly Standing Order			100.00
38	28/07/2015		Radcliff and Sons (PL01)	Supplier Payment	Chq No. 170015			660.00
39	28/07/2015		J Hollingham (SL01)	Customer Receipt	Chq No. 087651		2,675.52	
40	28/07/2015		Harry Bucket (SL04)	Customer Receipt	Chq No. 198871		500.00	
48	31/07/2015			Bank Payment	Bank Charge			32.19
49	31/07/2015			Bank Transfer	TRF01			432.16

Sports Gear

Detailed Nominal Activity: Cash in Hand (1210)
30 June, 2015 - 31 July, 2015

Transaction Type: All

Transaction number	Date	Invoice Number	Name	Type	Reference	Description	Debit	Credit
11	30/06/2015			Bank Opening Balance			300.00	
30	10/07/2015			Other Payment	Voucher No. 152			19.90
31	20/07/2015			Other Payment	Voucher No. 187			412.26
49	31/07/2015			Bank Transfer	TRF01		432.16	

PRACTICE PAPER 5

WAY TO WORK ANSWERS

TASK 3.3

Customer Address List

Way To Work

Customer Address List

Address Types: All

Customer Name	Address	Contact name	Phone	Mobile	Email	Fax
Morgan, Smith & Winston (JP01)	City Road Islington London N1 9PL United Kingdom	Main Contact				
Cyril West (JP02)	Grays West Grays Inn Road London WC1 1LP United Kingdom	Main Contact				
Wallace & Gromit Ltd (JP03)	134 Upper Street Islington London N1 2PT United Kingdom	Main Contact				
Star Paper (JP04)	66 White Lion Street London N1 5RX United Kingdom	Main Contact				

TASK 3.2

Supplier Address List

Way To Work

Supplier Address List

Address Types: All

Supplier Name	Address	Contact name	Phone	Mobile	Email	Fax
Paper Products Uk (SP01)	South Down Trading Estate Sheffield S15 4DR United Kingdom	Main Contact				
Wallace & Gromit Ltd (SP02)	134 Upper Street Islington London N1 2PT United Kingdom	Main Contact				
Whole Office Furniture (SP03)	176 East Way Leeds LD4 6PP United Kingdom	Main Contact				
Stationery World (SP04)	32 Great Portland Road London WC1V 6HH United Kingdom	Main Contact				

TASK 3.3

Trial Balance

Way To Work

Trial Balance Report

From Date: 28/02/2015   To Date: 31/03/2015

Nominal Code	Name	Debits	Credits
0040	Furniture and Fixtures - Cost	8,000.00	
0050	Motor Vehicles - Cost	14,000.00	
1100	Trade Debtors	9,173.68	
1200	Current	4,710.81	
1210	Cash in Hand	100.00	
1220	Deposit	1,500.00	
2100	Trade Creditors		18,535.76
3000	Capital		34,000.00
3260	Drawings	1,000.00	
4000	Stationery Sales		903.73
4001	CD Roms Sales		855.00
4002	Printer Accessories Sales		9,842.00
5000	Stationery Purchases	2,400.00	
5001	CD Rom Purchases	210.00	
5002	Printer Accessory Purchases	15,000.00	
7000	Wages and Salaries	5,600.00	
7100	Rent and rates	2,100.00	
8200	General Expenses	342.00	
	TOTAL	£64,136.49	£64,136.49

TASK 16

Customer Activity (detailed report)

Way To Work

Customer Activity Report

From Date: 28/02/2015

To Date: 31/03/2015

Morgan, Smith & Winston (JP01)

Date	Number	Reference	Type	Net	VAT	Total	Discount	Outstanding
28/02/2015		021	Customer OB Invoice	1,172.34	0.00	1,172.34		0.00
05/03/2015		INV043	Sales QE Invoice	4,376.00	875.20	5,251.20		5,251.20
07/03/2015		INV045	Sales QE Invoice	6,210.00	1,242.00	7,452.00		7,452.00
15/03/2015		Chq No. 203998	Customer Receipt			-1,172.34	0.00	0.00
						12,703.20		**12,703.20**

Cyril West (JP02)

Date	Number	Reference	Type	Net	VAT	Total	Discount	Outstanding
28/02/2015		045	Customer OB Invoice	2,954.00	0.00	2,954.00		0.00
03/03/2015		INV041	Sales QE Invoice	780.00	156.00	936.00		936.00
17/03/2015		Chq No. 103112	Customer Receipt			-2,954.00	0.00	0.00
						936.00		**936.00**

Wallace & Gromit Ltd (JP03)

Date	Number	Reference	Type	Net	VAT	Total	Discount	Outstanding
28/02/2015		033	Customer OB Invoice	3,180.00	0.00	3,180.00		3,180.00
07/03/2015		INV044	Sales QE Invoice	458.00	91.60	549.60		549.60
						3,729.60		**3,729.60**

Star Paper (JP04)

Date	Number	Reference	Type	Net	VAT	Total	Discount	Outstanding
28/02/2015		034	Customer OB Invoice	1,867.34	0.00	1,867.34		0.00
03/03/2015		INV042	Sales QE Invoice	921.00	184.20	1,105.20		1,105.20
17/03/2015		CR51	Sales QE Credit	-251.27	-50.25	-301.52		0.00
19/03/2015		Chq No. 011211	Customer Receipt			-1,565.82	0.00	0.00
						1,105.20		**1,105.20**

TASK 16

Supplier Activity (detailed report)

Way To Work

Supplier Activity Report

From Date: 28/02/2015

To Date: 31/03/2015

Paper Products Uk (SP01)

Date	Number	Reference	Type	Net	VAT	Total	Discount	Outstanding
28/02/2015		0165	Supplier OB Invoice	445.23	0.00	445.23		445.23
10/03/2015		0200	Purchase QE Invoice	489.00	97.80	586.80		586.80
31/03/2015		Chq No. 100076	Supplier Payment			-445.23		0.00
31/03/2015		Lost Chq - 100076	Supplier Refund			445.23		0.00
						1,032.03		1,032.03

Wallace & Gromit Ltd (SP02)

Date	Number	Reference	Type	Net	VAT	Total	Discount	Outstanding
28/02/2015		02183	Supplier OB Invoice	6,711.00	0.00	6,711.00		6,711.00
11/03/2015		02241	Purchase QE Invoice	345.00	69.00	414.00		414.00
						7,125.00		7,125.00

Whole Office Furniture (SP03)

Date	Number	Reference	Type	Net	VAT	Total	Discount	Outstanding
28/02/2015		1028	Supplier OB Invoice	1,875.21	0.00	1,875.21		0.00
11/03/2015		1098	Purchase QE Invoice	7,628.00	1,525.60	9,153.60		9,153.60
31/03/2015		Chq No. 100077	Supplier Payment			-1,875.21	0.00	0.00
						9,153.60		9,153.60

Stationery World (SP04)

Date	Number	Reference	Type	Net	VAT	Total	Discount	Outstanding
28/02/2015		0187	Supplier OB Invoice	9,504.32	0.00	9,504.32		0.00
14/03/2015		0197	Purchase QE Invoice	3,567.00	713.40	4,280.40		4,280.40
19/03/2015		RF287	Purchase QE Credit	-124.08	-24.82	-148.90		-148.90
31/03/2015		Chq No. 100078	Supplier Payment			-9,504.32	0.00	0.00
						4,131.50		4,131.50

TASK 16

Trial Balance

Way To Work

Trial Balance Report

From Date: 28/02/2015   To Date: 31/03/2015

Nominal Code	Name	Debits	Credits
0040	Furniture and Fixtures - Cost	8,000.00	
0050	Motor Vehicles - Cost	14,000.00	
1100	Trade Debtors	18,474.00	
1200	Current		2,144.53
1210	Cash in Hand	206.68	
1220	Deposit	1,500.00	
2100	Trade Creditors		21,442.13
2200	VAT on Sales		2,519.33
2201	VAT on Purchases	2,463.20	
3000	Capital		34,000.00
3260	Drawings	1,000.00	
4000	Stationery Sales		7,893.73
4001	CD Roms Sales		1,776.00
4002	Printer Accessories Sales		14,527.63
5000	Stationery Purchases	6,331.92	
5001	CD Rom Purchases	555.00	
5002	Printer Accessory Purchases	22,628.00	
6201	Advertising	327.00	
7000	Wages and Salaries	5,600.00	
7100	Rent and rates	2,668.00	
7200	Gas and electric	84.10	
7900	Bank charges and interest	123.45	
8200	General Expenses	342.00	
	TOTAL	£84,303.35	£84,303.35

TASK 16

Audit Trail for March (inc opening balances)

Way To Work

Audit Trail Breakdown

From Date: 28/02/2015

To Date: 31/03/2015

Type: All

Trans ID	Entry Date	Created By	Trans Date	Name	Type	Invoice Number	Ref	Ledger Account	Debit	Credit	Bank Reconciled	Deleted
1	01/06/2015	Sally Brummitt	28/02/2015	Morgan, Smith & Winston (JP01)	Customer OB Invoice		021	Opening Balances Control Account (9998)	0.00	1,172.34	No	No
1	01/06/2015	Sally Brummitt	28/02/2015	Morgan, Smith & Winston (JP01)	Customer OB Invoice		021	Trade Debtors (1100)	1,172.34	0.00	No	No
2	01/06/2015	Sally Brummitt	28/02/2015	Cyril West (JP02)	Customer OB Invoice		045	Opening Balances Control Account (9998)	0.00	2,954.00	No	No
2	01/06/2015	Sally Brummitt	28/02/2015	Cyril West (JP02)	Customer OB Invoice		045	Trade Debtors (1100)	2,954.00	0.00	No	No
3	01/06/2015	Sally Brummitt	28/02/2015	Wallace & Gromit Ltd (JP03)	Customer OB Invoice		033	Opening Balances Control Account (9998)	0.00	3,180.00	No	No
3	01/06/2015	Sally Brummitt	28/02/2015	Wallace & Gromit Ltd (JP03)	Customer OB Invoice		033	Trade Debtors (1100)	3,180.00	0.00	No	No

Mon 01 Jun 2015, 23:21

4	01/06/2015	Sally Brummitt	28/02/2015	Star Paper (JP04)	Customer OB Invoice		034	Opening Balances Control Account (9998)	0.00	1,867.34	No	No
4	01/06/2015	Sally Brummitt	28/02/2015	Star Paper (JP04)	Customer OB Invoice		034	Trade Debtors (1100)	1,867.34	0.00	No	No
5	01/06/2015	Sally Brummitt	28/02/2015	Paper Products Uk (SP01)	Supplier OB Invoice		0165	Opening Balances Control Account (9998)	445.23	0.00	No	No
5	01/06/2015	Sally Brummitt	28/02/2015	Paper Products Uk (SP01)	Supplier OB Invoice		0165	Trade Creditors (2100)	0.00	445.23	No	No
6	01/06/2015	Sally Brummitt	28/02/2015	Wallace & Gromit Ltd (SP02)	Supplier OB Invoice		02183	Opening Balances Control Account (9998)	12,000.00	0.00	No	Yes
6	01/06/2015	Sally Brummitt	28/02/2015	Wallace & Gromit Ltd (SP02)	Supplier OB Invoice		02183	Trade Creditors (2100)	0.00	12,000.00	No	Yes
6	01/06/2015	Sally Brummitt	28/02/2015	Wallace & Gromit Ltd (SP02)	Supplier OB Invoice		02183	Opening Balances Control Account (9998)	0.00	12,000.00	No	Yes
6	01/06/2015	Sally Brummitt	28/02/2015	Wallace & Gromit Ltd (SP02)	Supplier OB Invoice		02183	Trade Creditors (2100)	12,000.00	0.00	No	Yes
7	01/06/2015	Sally Brummitt	28/02/2015	Whole Office Furniture (SP03)	Supplier OB Invoice		1028	Opening Balances Control Account (9998)	1,875.21	0.00	No	No
7	01/06/2015	Sally Brummitt	28/02/2015	Whole Office Furniture (SP03)	Supplier OB Invoice		1028	Trade Creditors (2100)	0.00	1,875.21	No	No

Mon 01 Jun 2015, 23:21

8	01/06/2015	Sally Brummitt	28/02/2015	Wallace & Gromit Ltd (SP02)	Supplier OB Invoice	02183	Opening Balances Control Account (9998)	6,711.00	0.00	No	No
8	01/06/2015	Sally Brummitt	28/02/2015	Wallace & Gromit Ltd (SP02)	Supplier OB Invoice	02183	Trade Creditors (2100)	0.00	6,711.00	No	No
9	01/06/2015	Sally Brummitt	28/02/2015	Stationery World (SP04)	Supplier OB Invoice	0187	Opening Balances Control Account (9998)	9,504.32	0.00	No	No
9	01/06/2015	Sally Brummitt	28/02/2015	Stationery World (SP04)	Supplier OB Invoice	0187	Trade Creditors (2100)	0.00	9,504.32	No	No
10	01/06/2015	Sally Brummitt	28/02/2015		Bank Opening Balance		Opening Balances Control Account (9998)	0.00	6,210.81	No	No
10	01/06/2015	Sally Brummitt	28/02/2015		Bank Opening Balance		Current (1200)	6,210.81	0.00	Yes	No
11	01/06/2015	Sally Brummitt	28/02/2015		Bank Opening Balance		Opening Balances Control Account (9998)	0.00	100.00	No	No
11	01/06/2015	Sally Brummitt	28/02/2015		Bank Opening Balance		Cash in Hand (1210)	100.00	0.00	No	No
12	01/06/2015	Sally Brummitt	28/02/2015		Journal Opening Balance	O/Bal as 01/03/15	Motor Vehicles - Cost (0050)	14,000.00	0.00	No	No
12	01/06/2015	Sally Brummitt	28/02/2015		Journal Opening Balance	O/Bal as 01/03/15	Furniture and Fixtures - Cost (0040)	8,000.00	0.00	No	No
12	01/06/2015	Sally Brummitt	28/02/2015		Journal Opening Balance	O/Bal as 01/03/15	Opening Balances Control Account (9998)	34,000.00	0.00	No	No

12	01/06/2015	Sally Brummitt	28/02/2015		Journal Opening Balance	O/Bal as 01/03/15	Drawings (3260)	1,000.00	0.00	No	No
12	01/06/2015	Sally Brummitt	28/02/2015		Journal Opening Balance	O/Bal as 01/03/15	Opening Balances Control Account (9998)	903.73	0.00	No	No
12	01/06/2015	Sally Brummitt	28/02/2015		Journal Opening Balance	O/Bal as 01/03/15	Opening Balances Control Account (9998)	855.00	0.00	No	No
12	01/06/2015	Sally Brummitt	28/02/2015		Journal Opening Balance	O/Bal as 01/03/15	Opening Balances Control Account (9998)	9,842.00	0.00	No	No
12	01/06/2015	Sally Brummitt	28/02/2015		Journal Opening Balance	O/Bal as 01/03/15	Stationery Purchases (5000)	2,400.00	0.00	No	No
12	01/06/2015	Sally Brummitt	28/02/2015		Journal Opening Balance	O/Bal as 01/03/15	CD Rom Purchases (5001)	210.00	0.00	No	No
12	01/06/2015	Sally Brummitt	28/02/2015		Journal Opening Balance	O/Bal as 01/03/15	Printer Accessory Purchases (5002)	15,000.00	0.00	No	No
12	01/06/2015	Sally Brummitt	28/02/2015		Journal Opening Balance	O/Bal as 01/03/15	Wages and Salaries (7000)	5,600.00	0.00	No	No
12	01/06/2015	Sally Brummitt	28/02/2015		Journal Opening Balance	O/Bal as 01/03/15	General Expenses (8200)	342.00	0.00	No	No
12	01/06/2015	Sally Brummitt	28/02/2015		Journal Opening Balance	O/Bal as 01/03/15	Rent and rates (7100)	2,100.00	0.00	No	No
12	01/06/2015	Sally Brummitt	28/02/2015		Journal Opening Balance	O/Bal as 01/03/15	Opening Balances Control Account (9998)	0.00	14,000.00	Yes	No
12	01/06/2015	Sally Brummitt	28/02/2015		Journal Opening Balance	O/Bal as 01/03/15	Opening Balances Control Account (9998)	0.00	8,000.00	No	No

No	Date	User	Date	Name	Type	Ref	Account	Debit	Credit		
12	01/06/2015	Sally Brummitt	28/02/2015		Journal Opening Balance	O/Bal as 01/03/15	Capital (3000)	0.00	34,000.00	No	No
12	01/06/2015	Sally Brummitt	28/02/2015		Journal Opening Balance	O/Bal as 01/03/15	Opening Balances Control Account (9998)	0.00	1,000.00	No	No
12	01/06/2015	Sally Brummitt	28/02/2015		Journal Opening Balance	O/Bal as 01/03/15	Stationery Sales (4000)	0.00	903.73	No	No
12	01/06/2015	Sally Brummitt	28/02/2015		Journal Opening Balance	O/Bal as 01/03/15	CD Roms Sales (4001)	0.00	855.00	No	No
12	01/06/2015	Sally Brummitt	28/02/2015		Journal Opening Balance	O/Bal as 01/03/15	Printer Accessories Sales (4002)	0.00	9,842.00	No	No
12	01/06/2015	Sally Brummitt	28/02/2015		Journal Opening Balance	O/Bal as 01/03/15	Opening Balances Control Account (9998)	0.00	2,400.00	No	No
12	01/06/2015	Sally Brummitt	28/02/2015		Journal Opening Balance	O/Bal as 01/03/15	Opening Balances Control Account (9998)	0.00	210.00	No	No
12	01/06/2015	Sally Brummitt	28/02/2015		Journal Opening Balance	O/Bal as 01/03/15	Opening Balances Control Account (9998)	0.00	15,000.00	No	No
12	01/06/2015	Sally Brummitt	28/02/2015		Journal Opening Balance	O/Bal as 01/03/15	Opening Balances Control Account (9998)	0.00	5,600.00	No	No
12	01/06/2015	Sally Brummitt	28/02/2015		Journal Opening Balance	O/Bal as 01/03/15	Opening Balances Control Account (9998)	0.00	342.00	No	No
12	01/06/2015	Sally Brummitt	28/02/2015		Journal Opening Balance	O/Bal as 01/03/15	Opening Balances Control Account (9998)	0.00	2,100.00	No	No

No	Date	User	Date	Name	Type	Ref	Account	Debit	Credit		
13	01/06/2015	Sally Brummitt	01/03/2015		Bank Transfer	TRANS01	Current (1200)	0.00	1,500.00	Yes	No
13	01/06/2015	Sally Brummitt	01/03/2015		Bank Transfer	TRANS01	Deposit (1220)	1,500.00	0.00	No	No
14	01/06/2015	Sally Brummitt	03/03/2015	Cyril West (JP02)	Sales QE Invoice	INV041	Stationery Sales (4000)	0.00	780.00	No	No
14	01/06/2015	Sally Brummitt	03/03/2015	Cyril West (JP02)	Sales QE Invoice	INV041	VAT on Sales (2200)	0.00	156.00	No	No
14	01/06/2015	Sally Brummitt	03/03/2015	Cyril West (JP02)	Sales QE Invoice	INV041	Trade Debtors (1100)	936.00	0.00	No	No
15	01/06/2015	Sally Brummitt	03/03/2015	Star Paper (JP04)	Sales QE Invoice	INV042	CD Roms Sales (4001)	0.00	921.00	No	No
15	01/06/2015	Sally Brummitt	03/03/2015	Star Paper (JP04)	Sales QE Invoice	INV042	VAT on Sales (2200)	0.00	184.20	No	No
15	01/06/2015	Sally Brummitt	03/03/2015	Star Paper (JP04)	Sales QE Invoice	INV042	Trade Debtors (1100)	1,105.20	0.00	No	No
16	01/06/2015	Sally Brummitt	05/03/2015	Morgan, Smith & Winston (JP01)	Sales QE Invoice	INV043	Printer Accessories Sales (4002)	0.00	4,376.00	No	No
16	01/06/2015	Sally Brummitt	05/03/2015	Morgan, Smith & Winston (JP01)	Sales QE Invoice	INV043	VAT on Sales (2200)	0.00	875.20	No	No
16	01/06/2015	Sally Brummitt	05/03/2015	Morgan, Smith & Winston (JP01)	Sales QE Invoice	INV043	Trade Debtors (1100)	5,251.20	0.00	No	No
17	01/06/2015	Sally Brummitt	07/03/2015	Wallace & Gromit Ltd (JP03)	Sales QE Invoice	INV044	Printer Accessories Sales (4002)	0.00	458.00	No	No
17	01/06/2015	Sally Brummitt	07/03/2015	Wallace & Gromit Ltd (JP03)	Sales QE Invoice	INV044	VAT on Sales (2200)	0.00	91.60	No	No
17	01/06/2015	Sally Brummitt	07/03/2015	Wallace & Gromit Ltd (JP03)	Sales QE Invoice	INV044	Trade Debtors (1100)	549.60	0.00	No	No

18	01/06/2015	Sally Brummitt	07/03/2015	Morgan, Smith & Winston (JP01)	Sales QE Invoice	INV045	Stationery Sales (4000)	0.00	6,210.00	No	No
18	01/06/2015	Sally Brummitt	07/03/2015	Morgan, Smith & Winston (JP01)	Sales QE Invoice	INV045	VAT on Sales (2200)	0.00	1,242.00	No	No
18	01/06/2015	Sally Brummitt	07/03/2015	Morgan, Smith & Winston (JP01)	Sales QE Invoice	INV045	Trade Debtors (1100)	7,452.00	0.00	No	No
19	01/06/2015	Sally Brummitt	17/03/2015	Star Paper (JP04)	Sales QE Credit	CR51	Trade Debtors (1100)	0.00	301.52	No	No
19	01/06/2015	Sally Brummitt	17/03/2015	Star Paper (JP04)	Sales QE Credit	CR51	Printer Accessories Sales (4002)	251.27	0.00	No	No
19	01/06/2015	Sally Brummitt	17/03/2015	Star Paper (JP04)	Sales QE Credit	CR51	VAT on Sales (2200)	50.25	0.00	No	No
20	01/06/2015	Sally Brummitt	10/03/2015	Paper Products Uk (SP01)	Purchase QE Invoice	0200	Stationery Purchases (5000)	489.00	0.00	No	No
20	01/06/2015	Sally Brummitt	10/03/2015	Paper Products Uk (SP01)	Purchase QE Invoice	0200	VAT on Purchases (2201)	97.80	0.00	No	No
20	01/06/2015	Sally Brummitt	10/03/2015	Paper Products Uk (SP01)	Purchase QE Invoice	0200	Trade Creditors (2100)	0.00	586.80	No	No
21	01/06/2015	Sally Brummitt	11/03/2015	Wallace & Gromit Ltd (SP02)	Purchase QE Invoice	02241	CD Rom Purchases (5001)	345.00	0.00	No	No
21	01/06/2015	Sally Brummitt	11/03/2015	Wallace & Gromit Ltd (SP02)	Purchase QE Invoice	02241	VAT on Purchases (2201)	69.00	0.00	No	No
21	01/06/2015	Sally Brummitt	11/03/2015	Wallace & Gromit Ltd (SP02)	Purchase QE Invoice	02241	Trade Creditors (2100)	0.00	414.00	No	No

22	01/06/2015	Sally Brummitt	11/03/2015	Whole Office Furniture (SP03)	Purchase QE Invoice	1098	Printer Accessory Purchases (5002)	7,628.00	0.00	No	No
22	01/06/2015	Sally Brummitt	11/03/2015	Whole Office Furniture (SP03)	Purchase QE Invoice	1098	VAT on Purchases (2201)	1,525.60	0.00	No	No
22	01/06/2015	Sally Brummitt	11/03/2015	Whole Office Furniture (SP03)	Purchase QE Invoice	1098	Trade Creditors (2100)	0.00	9,153.60	No	No
23	01/06/2015	Sally Brummitt	14/03/2015	Stationery World (SP04)	Purchase QE Invoice	0197	Stationery Purchases (5000)	3,567.00	0.00	No	No
23	01/06/2015	Sally Brummitt	14/03/2015	Stationery World (SP04)	Purchase QE Invoice	0197	VAT on Purchases (2201)	713.40	0.00	No	No
23	01/06/2015	Sally Brummitt	14/03/2015	Stationery World (SP04)	Purchase QE Invoice	0197	Trade Creditors (2100)	0.00	4,280.40	No	No
24	01/06/2015	Sally Brummitt	19/03/2015	Stationery World (SP04)	Purchase QE Credit	RF287	Trade Creditors (2100)	148.90	0.00	No	No
24	01/06/2015	Sally Brummitt	19/03/2015	Stationery World (SP04)	Purchase QE Credit	RF287	Stationery Purchases (5000)	0.00	124.08	No	No
24	01/06/2015	Sally Brummitt	19/03/2015	Stationery World (SP04)	Purchase QE Credit	RF287	VAT on Purchases (2201)	0.00	24.82	No	No
25	01/06/2015	Sally Brummitt	15/03/2015	Morgan, Smith & Winston (JP01)	Customer Receipt	Chq No. 203998	Current (1200)	1,172.34	0.00	Yes	No
25	01/06/2015	Sally Brummitt	15/03/2015	Morgan, Smith & Winston (JP01)	Customer Receipt	Chq No. 203998	Trade Debtors (1100)	0.00	1,172.34	No	No
26	01/06/2015	Sally Brummitt	17/03/2015	Cyril West (JP02)	Customer Receipt	Chq No. 103112	Current (1200)	2,954.00	0.00	Yes	No
26	01/06/2015	Sally Brummitt	17/03/2015	Cyril West (JP02)	Customer Receipt	Chq No. 103112	Trade Debtors (1100)	0.00	2,954.00	No	No
27	01/06/2015	Sally Brummitt	19/03/2015	Star Paper (JP04)	Customer Receipt	Chq No. 011211	Trade Debtors (1100)	301.52	0.00	No	No

27	01/06/2015	Sally Brummitt	19/03/2015	Star Paper (JP04)	Customer Receipt	Chq No. 011211	Current (1200)	1,565.82	0.00	Yes	No
27	01/06/2015	Sally Brummitt	19/03/2015	Star Paper (JP04)	Customer Receipt	Chq No. 011211	Trade Debtors (1100)	0.00	1,867.34	No	No
28	01/06/2015	Sally Brummitt	31/03/2015	Paper Products Uk (SP01)	Supplier Payment	Chq No. 100076	Trade Creditors (2100)	445.23	0.00	No	Yes
28	01/06/2015	Sally Brummitt	31/03/2015	Paper Products Uk (SP01)	Supplier Payment	Chq No. 100076	Current (1200)	0.00	445.23	No	Yes
28	01/06/2015	Sally Brummitt	31/03/2015	Paper Products Uk (SP01)	Supplier Payment	Chq No. 100076	Trade Creditors (2100)	0.00	445.23	No	Yes
28	01/06/2015	Sally Brummitt	31/03/2015	Paper Products Uk (SP01)	Supplier Payment	Chq No. 100076	Current (1200)	445.23	0.00	No	Yes
29	01/06/2015	Sally Brummitt	31/03/2015	Whole Office Furniture (SP03)	Supplier Payment	Chq No. 100077	Trade Creditors (2100)	1,875.21	0.00	No	No
29	01/06/2015	Sally Brummitt	31/03/2015	Whole Office Furniture (SP03)	Supplier Payment	Chq No. 100077	Current (1200)	0.00	1,875.21	Yes	No
30	01/06/2015	Sally Brummitt	31/03/2015	Stationery World (SP04)	Supplier Payment	Chq No. 100078	Trade Creditors (2100)	9,504.32	0.00	No	No
30	01/06/2015	Sally Brummitt	31/03/2015	Stationery World (SP04)	Supplier Payment	Chq No. 100078	Current (1200)	0.00	9,504.32	No	No
31	01/06/2015	Sally Brummitt	15/03/2015		Bank Transfer	TRANS02	Current (1200)	0.00	600.00	Yes	No
31	01/06/2015	Sally Brummitt	15/03/2015		Bank Transfer	TRANS02	Cash in Hand (1210)	600.00	0.00	No	No
32	01/06/2015	Sally Brummitt	19/03/2015		Other Payment	056	Cash in Hand (1210)	0.00	100.92	No	No
32	01/06/2015	Sally Brummitt	19/03/2015		Other Payment	056	Gas and electric (7200)	84.10	0.00	No	No

32	01/06/2015	Sally Brummitt	19/03/2015		Other Payment	056	VAT on Purchases (2201)	16.82	0.00	No	No
33	01/06/2015	Sally Brummitt	20/03/2015		Other Payment	057	Cash in Hand (1210)	0.00	392.40	No	No
33	01/06/2015	Sally Brummitt	20/03/2015		Other Payment	057	Advertising (6201)	327.00	0.00	No	No
33	01/06/2015	Sally Brummitt	20/03/2015		Other Payment	057	VAT on Purchases (2201)	65.40	0.00	No	No
34	01/06/2015	Sally Brummitt	28/03/2015		Other Receipt	ST4	Printer Accessories Sales (4002)	0.00	102.90	No	No
34	01/06/2015	Sally Brummitt	28/03/2015		Other Receipt	ST4	VAT on Sales (2200)	0.00	20.58	No	No
34	01/06/2015	Sally Brummitt	28/03/2015		Other Receipt	ST4	Current (1200)	123.48	0.00	Yes	No
35	01/06/2015	Sally Brummitt	31/03/2015	Paper Products Uk (SP01)	Supplier Payment	Chq No. 100076	Trade Creditors (2100)	445.23	0.00	No	No
35	01/06/2015	Sally Brummitt	31/03/2015	Paper Products Uk (SP01)	Supplier Payment	Chq No. 100076	Current (1200)	0.00	445.23	Yes	No
36	01/06/2015	Sally Brummitt	31/03/2015	Paper Products Uk (SP01)	Supplier Refund	Lost Chq - 100076	Current (1200)	445.23	0.00	Yes	No
36	01/06/2015	Sally Brummitt	31/03/2015	Paper Products Uk (SP01)	Supplier Refund	Lost Chq - 100076	Trade Creditors (2100)	0.00	445.23	No	No
37	01/06/2015	Sally Brummitt	31/03/2015		Other Payment	Monthly Standing Order	Current (1200)	0.00	568.00	No	Yes
37	01/06/2015	Sally Brummitt	31/03/2015		Other Payment	Monthly Standing Order	Rent and rates (7100)	568.00	0.00	No	Yes
37	01/06/2015	Sally Brummitt	31/03/2015		Other Payment	Monthly Standing Order	VAT on Purchases (2201)	0.00	0.00	No	Yes

37	01/06/2015	Sally Brummitt	31/03/2015		Other Payment	Monthly Standing Order	Current (1200)	568.00	0.00	No	Yes
37	01/06/2015	Sally Brummitt	31/03/2015		Other Payment	Monthly Standing Order	Rent and rates (7100)	0.00	568.00	No	Yes
37	01/06/2015	Sally Brummitt	31/03/2015		Other Payment	Monthly Standing Order	VAT on Purchases (2201)	0.00	0.00	No	Yes
38	01/06/2015	Sally Brummitt	31/03/2015		Other Payment	Monthly Standing Order	Current (1200)	0.00	568.00	Yes	No
38	01/06/2015	Sally Brummitt	31/03/2015		Other Payment	Monthly Standing Order	Rent and rates (7100)	568.00	0.00	No	No
38	01/06/2015	Sally Brummitt	31/03/2015		Other Payment	Monthly Standing Order	VAT on Purchases (2201)	0.00	0.00	No	No
41	01/06/2015	Sally Brummitt	31/03/2015		Bank Payment	Bank Charge	Current (1200)	0.00	123.45	Yes	No
41	01/06/2015	Sally Brummitt	31/03/2015		Bank Payment	Bank Charge	Bank charges and interest (7900)	123.45	0.00	No	No

TASK 16

Nominal Ledger Activity for Bank/Petty Cash

Way To Work

Detailed Nominal Activity: Current (1200)

28 February, 2015 - 31 March, 2015

Transaction Type: All

Transaction number	Date	Invoice Number	Name	Type	Reference	Description	Debit	Credit
10	28/02/2015			Bank Opening Balance			6,210.81	
13	01/03/2015			Bank Transfer	TRANS01			1,500.00
25	15/03/2015		Morgan, Smith & Winston (JP01)	Customer Receipt	Chq No. 203998		1,172.34	
31	15/03/2015			Bank Transfer	TRANS02			600.00
26	17/03/2015		Cyril West (JP02)	Customer Receipt	Chq No. 103112		2,954.00	
27	19/03/2015		Star Paper (JP04)	Customer Receipt	Chq No. 011211		1,565.82	
34	28/03/2015			Other Receipt	ST4		123.48	
35	31/03/2015		Paper Products Uk (SP01)	Supplier Payment	Chq No. 100076			445.23
36	31/03/2015		Paper Products Uk (SP01)	Supplier Refund	Lost Chq - 100076		445.23	
38	31/03/2015			Other Payment	Monthly Standing Order			568.00
29	31/03/2015		Whole Office Furniture (SP03)	Supplier Payment	Chq No. 100077			1,875.21
41	31/03/2015			Bank Payment	Bank Charge			123.45
30	31/03/2015		Stationery World (SP04)	Supplier Payment	Chq No. 100078			9,504.32

KAPLAN PUBLISHING

Way To Work

Detailed Nominal Activity: Cash in Hand (1210)

28 February, 2015 - 31 March, 2015

Transaction Type: All

Transaction number	Date	Invoice Number	Name	Type	Reference	Description	Debit	Credit
11	28/02/2015			Bank Opening Balance				100.00
31	15/03/2015			Bank Transfer	TRANS02		600.00	
32	19/03/2015			Other Payment	056			100.92
33	20/03/2015			Other Payment	057			392.40

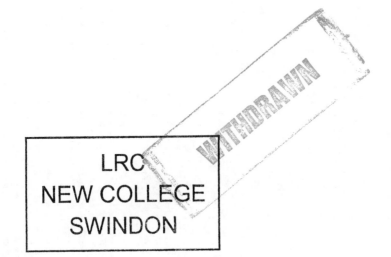

KAPLAN PUBLISHING